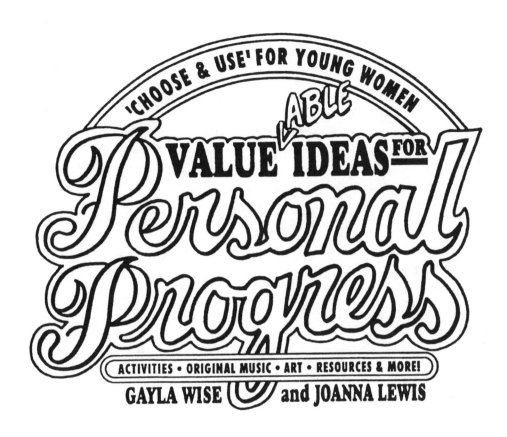

'CHOOSE & USE' FOR YOUNG WOMEN

VALUE-ABLE IDEAS FOR *Personal Progress*

ACTIVITIES • ORIGINAL MUSIC • ART • RESOURCES & MORE!

GAYLA WISE and JOANNA LEWIS

94 95 96 97 98 99 00 01   10 9 8 7 6 5 4 3

Library of Congress Catalog Number: 92-073587
Value-able Ideas for Personal Progress
Covenant Communications, Inc.
ISBN 1-55503-422-5

How to Use this Book

Today's Young Women are choice daughters of our Heavenly Father. This book is for them and their leaders. The "value-able" ideas in this book are designed to integrate the Young Women values and the Personal Progress goals into experiences that are both fun and worthwhile.

Experiences

Ardeth Kapp said, "We equate 'activities' with fun and games and entertainment—things that cost money. If we use the term 'experiences' we think about things related to the mission of the Church . . . to experiences that provide opportunities to practice gospel principles learned on Sunday." ("A Time to Gather," talk given Oct. 1990.) For this reason, we use the word "experiences" to refer to the value-related ideas discussed. These events will give the girls enjoyable hands-on experience using the Young Women values and gospel principles.

Art

The art in this book is designed to be photocopied and used in a variety of ways to help make the planning and preparation of your Young Women events easy, attractive, and successful.

1. Some pieces of art are small enough that more than one will fit on a page. This allows you to make multiple copies quickly. For example, if three invitations will fit on one page, make three copies, cut these invitations apart, and tape them onto one page. Make your copies from this master page.

2. Some art, such as the invitations, include lines and spaces for you to fill in information. To use these, make one copy, write in your information with a black ink pen, and then make your copies from this master copy.

3. All art in this book is usable, even art that contains text. If you do not want to include the text, simply make one copy, white out or cut out the text on this copy, and photocopy it to make your master copy.

4. All art can be reduced or enlarged to use as visual aids. You can make large or small posters, handouts, cutout decorations, invitations, reminders, Personal Progress pages, etc.

Lesson and Music Resources

Use the lesson and music resources to help you find Church-approved supplemental material to teach the Young Women values.

Songs

Use the original songs included at the end of each value section to help instill the Young Women values in the hearts of your girls. Nearly every song included is written by a different composer in order to provide the musician with a variety of style, appeal, usage, and level of playing difficulty.

This book will help make your Young Women experiences easy, "value-able," and successful. Be creative and enjoy watching your girls make Personal Progress.

Be Creative

Art, including pictures and borders, may be photocopied from anywhere in the book and adapted to specific uses. Examples of possible uses are shown below.

Make an invitation to the Mock Jury Trial (under Integrity) using the following art:

1. The border from the "Worth of a Widow" journal page (under Individual Worth), p. 39.
2. The scales from the Integrity chapter title page.

Make an invitation to the guitar night (under Knowledge) using the following art:

1. The border from the invitation to the "Individual Worth Cookies" activity, p. 36.
2. The guitar from the "Guitar" section (under Knowledge), p. 48.

Welcome home a missionary, a college student, or a friend who has been in the hospital, using the following art:

1. The house from the Choice and Accountability chapter title page.
2. A border from one of the chapter title pages.

Make a reminder for a song rehearsal using the following art:

1. The border from the Car Window Wash cards (under Good Works), p. 75.
2. The hearts from the Music Resources page in the Knowledge section, p. 53.

Make a gift tag for a plate of cookies using the cookie from "Individual Worth Cookies," p. 36.

CONTENTS

Faith

I am a daughter of a Heavenly Father who loves me, and I will have faith in his eternal plan, which centers in Jesus Christ, my Savior.

1. Thou shalt have no other gods before me.

2. Thou shalt not make unto thee any graven image.

3. Thou shalt not take the name of the Lord thy God in vain.

4. Remember the sabbath day, to keep it holy.

5. Honour thy father and thy mother.

6. Thou shalt not kill.

7. Thou shalt not commit adultery.

8. Thou shalt not steal.

9. Thou shalt not bear false witness.

10. Thou shalt not covet.

"And, if you keep my commandments and endure to the end you shall have eternal life, which gift is the greatest of all the gifts of God."

D&C 14:7

Faith
Campfire

OBJECTIVE:

For girls to feel close to one another and to feel the Spirit.

PREPARATION:

- Make arrangements for food, campfire, and transportation.
- Ask the girls to prepare to share a faith-promoting story.

PROCEDURE:

Cook dinner over a campfire, preferably in a secluded location. Set a quiet mood by singing a familiar song, such as "Listen to the Still, Small Voice." Have every girl share a personal story or a family story of faith so the Spirit will touch their hearts. At the conclusion, point out that the tender feelings they have felt are whisperings from the Spirit that help their faith grow.

ALTERNATIVES:

Gather the girls around the campfire to enjoy a testimony meeting. Ask each girl to write down on a slip of paper something she needs to overcome. At the end of the program, the girls throw the slips of paper into the fire to symbolize overcoming the challenge or temptation. Or each girl can toss a pinecone into the fire with the same symbolism in mind.

PERSONAL PROGRESS GOALS:

Beehive 1, Faith #1 and #8; Mia Maid 1, Faith #2; Mia Maid 2, Faith #4.

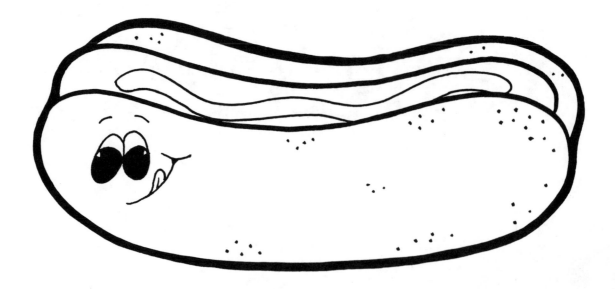

Faith

Missionary Moments

OBJECTIVE:

To strengthen the girls' faith by acquainting them with missionaries and missionary teachings.

PREPARATION:

- Invite four stake missionaries to each teach a class on missionary work and to bring missionary pamphlets.
- Assign the girls to bring scriptures.

PROCEDURE:

Set up four workshops, each led by one missionary:

1. Beehive 1—The missionary discusses ways girls and their families can do missionary work. Each girl chooses one way and lists steps she will follow to fulfill this goal. After her experience, she reports to the missionaries.

2. Beehive 2—The missionary teaches scriptures used to teach nonmembers about faith. The girls memorize three scriptures, repeat them to their advisor, and explain what they mean.

3. Mia Maid 1—After distributing two missionary pamphlets to each girl, the missionary teaches briefly about each pamphlet. Girls choose partners and teach each other what they have learned.

4. Mia Maid 2—The missionary teaches girls the first discussion. Girls are to repeat this lesson to a family member or a friend at a later time. Or the missionary teaches the lesson in segments and then the girls teach each other before continuing. The first exercise allows the missionary to teach the complete lesson; the second gives the girls the opportunity to immediately practice what they learned.

PERSONAL PROGRESS GOALS:

Beehive 1, Faith #3; Beehive 2, Faith #4; Mia Maid 1, Faith #5; Mia Maid 2, Faith #6.

Faith

Scripture Seeds

OBJECTIVE:

To compare faith to seeds that must be planted and nurtured.

PREPARATION:

- Assign each girl to bring scriptures, lined paper, pen, and scissors.
- Make up one seed packet for each girl (see the following page).
- Obtain mustard seeds.

PROCEDURE:

1. Group the girls into teams. Working individually, each girl uses the topical guide to find a different scripture on faith. She writes it on lined paper using every other line so the words can be cut apart. These words are scripture "seeds." Then the girls put the seeds they have cut apart into "seed packets" and label the packets with the scripture reference.

2. Have the teams trade seed packets. Working together as a team and without looking up the references, the girls try to put the words into the proper order. In a sense, as the girls complete each packet, the seeds "grow" into full-size scriptures.

3. Ask each girl to select and memorize one of the scriptures. Compare this process to "planting" the scripture seed in their own lives.

4. Be creative. Let each team choose one scripture and come up with a Mormonad for it. They may want to submit the best one to the *New Era*.

5. Teach the song "The Seed Within Your Heart," found at the end of this chapter.

SUGGESTED READINGS:

1. "Know Your 'Rights,'" Jacob de Jager, *New Era*, Mar. 1991, pp. 4-7. In a dream, an angel is a salesclerk in the mall. He sells anything one wants but only in the form of seeds. (See Alma 32:41-43.)

2. "The Net Result," Guy Fitzgerald, *New Era*, Oct. 1991, pp. 10-11. The youth can plant seeds of faith by their example to nonmembers.

3. The parable of the mustard seed (Matthew 13:31-32; see also Matthew 17:20). Give each girl a mustard seed. They may want to plant the seeds at home.

PERSONAL PROGRESS GOALS:

Beehive 1, Faith #4; Beehive 2, Faith #8; Mia Maid 1, Faith #1 and #7; Mia Maid 2, Faith #5.

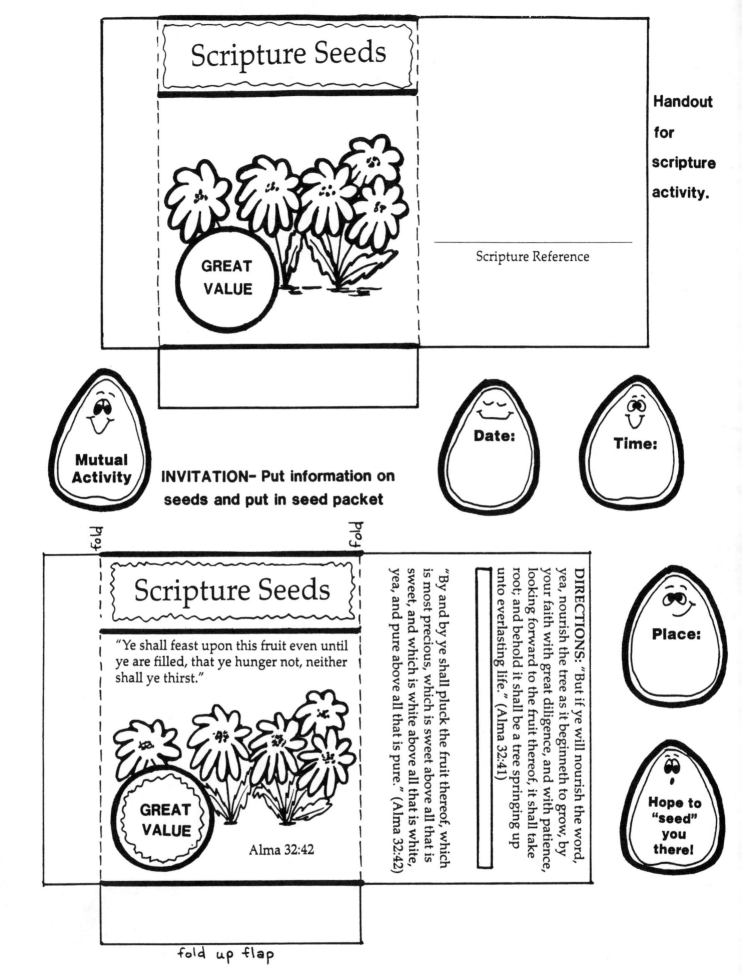

Scripture Seeds

GREAT VALUE

Handout for scripture activity.

_____
Scripture Reference

Mutual Activity

INVITATION- Put information on seeds and put in seed packet

Date:

Time:

Place:

Hope to "seed" you there!

fold

fold

Scripture Seeds

"Ye shall feast upon this fruit even until ye are filled, that ye hunger not, neither shall ye thirst."

GREAT VALUE

Alma 32:42

"By and by ye shall pluck the fruit thereof, which is most precious, which is sweet above all that is sweet, and which is white above all that is white, yea, and pure above all that is pure." (Alma 32:42)

DIRECTIONS: "But if ye will nourish the word, yea, nourish the tree as it beginneth to grow, by your faith with great diligence, and with patience, looking forward to the fruit thereof, it shall take root; and behold it shall be a tree springing up unto everlasting life." (Alma 32:41)

fold up flap

Faith

Sunday Night Discussions

OBJECTIVE:

To teach newly converted and recently activated girls basic gospel teachings. All girls are invited.

PREPARATION:

- Request that the bishopric call a specialist to teach weekly discussions.
- Obtain a *Gospel Principles* manual.*
- Arrange for a home to meet in each Sunday evening.
- Photocopy the next page so that it measures 11" x 17" and use it as a poster to invite the Young Women to the discussions. Tape strips of paper next to the words *time*, *place*, and *topic* so you can change this information each week.

PROCEDURE:

Teach one of the following lessons each week (all except number 9 are from *Gospel Principles*):

1. Pre-Earth Life, chapters 1 and 2.
2. The Mission of Jesus Christ, chapter 3.
3. The Life of Christ, chapter 11.
4. The Atonement, chapter 12.
5. Faith, chapter 18.
6. Prayer, chapter 8.
7. Repentance, chapter 19.
8. The Holy Ghost, chapters 7 and 21.
9. Joseph Smith, the Prophet, and the Book of Mormon. See "Joseph, the Seer," Spiritual Living Lesson #22 and "The Book of Mormon Is the Word of God," Spiritual Living Lesson #2. Both lessons are in the *Come Unto Me* Relief Society Personal Study Guide 1988. (Note: the reprint edition, Study Guide 3, does not contain these lessons.)
10. Life After Death, chapters 45 and 46.

EXAMPLE:

In one Young Women's program, these discussions filled a basic need for the girls, who grew in both faith and gospel knowledge. They asked for an additional discussion on the Second Coming of Christ (*Gospel Principles*, chapters 41 and 43). On the last evening, they shared how they felt about what they had learned. In a non-threatening, informal setting, they each bore their testimonies without realizing they had done so.

PERSONAL PROGRESS GOALS:

Beehive 2, Faith #7, Divine Nature #3 and #4, and Choice and Accountability #1; Mia Maid 1, Faith #1, #2, #8, and #9; Mia Maid 2, Faith #4, Divine Nature #5, and Choice and Accountability #7.

---

* Available from Church distribution. See page 109 of this book for details.

HEAR YE! HEAR YE!

REMINDER:

SUNDAY NIGHT DISCUSSION

It's Tonight!

Time:

Place:

Topic:

See You There!

Faith

Testimony Dinner

OBJECTIVE:

For the girls to feel the Spirit and share their testimonies.

PREPARATION:

- Invite the full-time missionaries.
- Assign girls to bring food, to set up, and to clean up.
- Encourage each girl to set a Personal Progress goal to share her testimony.
- Make copies of the bookmark on the following page for the girls.

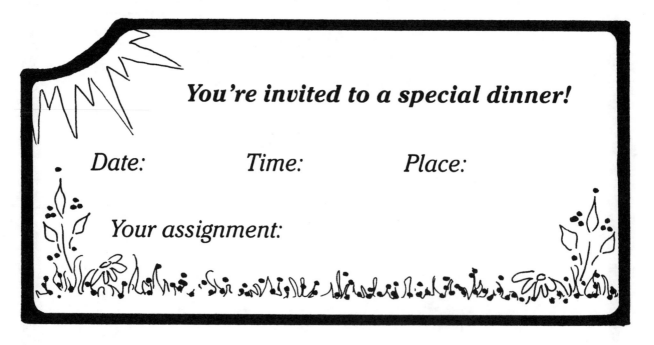

You're invited to a special dinner!

Date: Time: Place:

Your assignment:

PROCEDURE:

Invite the full-time missionaries to a dinner that the girls prepare. Have the missionaries give talks on what a testimony is, how to gain one, and how to keep and strengthen it. Both of them should talk about testimonies and bear their testimonies. Ask each girl to share her feelings about the gospel by answering this question: "What principle of the gospel is important to you today?" This setting allows the girls to respond easily. Point out at the conclusion that those who have shared their feelings have actually borne their testimonies.

SUGGESTED READINGS:

1. The story of the young woman in "To Some It Is Given," Jenae P. Miller, *Ensign*, Jan. 1992, pp. 30-31. She struggled for a testimony to discover that she already accepted gospel truths.
2. President David O. McKay's personal experience of praying for a testimony (quoted on following the page).

"I realized in youth that the most precious thing that a man could obtain in this life was a testimony of the divinity of this work. I hungered for it. . . . I remember riding over the hills one afternoon, thinking of these things, and concluded that there in the silence of the hills was the best place to get that testimony. I stopped my horse . . . and knelt by the side of a tree.

"With all the fervor of my heart [I] poured out my soul to God and asked him for a testimony of this gospel. I had in mind that there would be some manifestation, that I should receive some transformation that would leave me without doubt.

"I arose, mounted my horse, and as he started over the trail I remember rather introspectively searching myself, and involuntarily shaking my head, said to myself, 'No sir, there is no change; I am just the same boy I was before I knelt down.' The anticipated manifestation had not come.

"Nor was that the only occasion. However, it did come, but not in the way I had anticipated. . . . The testimony that this work is divine [came], not through manifestation . . . but through obedience to God's will, in harmony with Christ's promise, 'If any man will do his will, he will know of the doctrine, whether it be of God.' (John 7:17)." ("A Personal Testimony," *The Improvement Era*, Sept. 1962, pp. 628-629.)

EXAMPLE:

A leader who held a testimony dinner made this comment, "It was very spiritual. The girls were greatly strengthened."

PERSONAL PROGRESS GOALS:

Mia Maid 2, Faith #4. A good optional goal is Mia Maid 1, Faith #2.

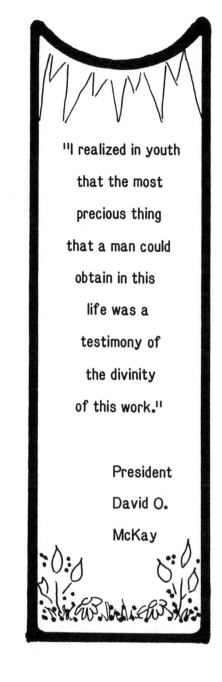

"I realized in youth that the most precious thing that a man could obtain in this life was a testimony of the divinity of this work."

President David O. McKay

Faith

Lesson Resources

ARTICLES

"A Change of Heart," Christie Ann Giles, *New Era*, Nov. 1991, p. 11. The author learned the difference between saying a prayer and praying.

"Following in His Footsteps," Rachel Rackham, *New Era*, May 1992, pp. 14-15. Following her dad up the canyon in the dark, Rachel learned about faith.

"Harmer Accidents," Vivian Harmer, *New Era*, Aug. 1985, pp. 16-19. A crisis restored her faith in a prayer that had previously seemed trite.

"I Found Out for Myself," Robert J. Cutter, *New Era*, Apr. 1991, pp. 12-14. One friend balked at the Church while another stood up for it.

"Just Try to Stop Me!" Ashley Moran, *New Era*, Nov. 1991, pp. 12-14. A teenager received an answer that the Church is true and joined in spite of opposition.

"Letters from Home," Ardeth G. Kapp, *New Era*, Nov. 1988, pp. 9-11. A challenge to renew commitment to regular scripture reading.

"Opposite Reaction," Stephanie Radford, *New Era*, Oct. 1991, p. 9. Anti-Mormon flyers spurred her to study the scriptures and strengthen her faith.

"Q&A: How Can I Gain a Testimony?" *New Era*, Sept. 1989, pp. 16-19.

"Q&A: How Can I Tell the Promptings of the Spirit?" *New Era*, Mar. 1989, pp. 17-19.

"The Burning Came Later," H. Allan Lawrence, *New Era*, May 1991, p. 9. The simple realization that he knew came into his mind.

"The Elusive Balance," Glenn L. Pace, *New Era*, Mar. 1989, pp. 44-50. We can learn how to recognize and obtain personal revelation.

"The Eye of Faith," Robert B. Harbertson, *New Era*, Sept. 1988, pp. 4-7. Faith includes doing all we can to bring the desired result.

"The Next Fifteen Minutes," Robert L. Simpson, *New Era*, July 1989, pp. 4-6. A deacon devastated by anti-Mormon ideas received an answer to his prayer for help.

"Time Trial," Lisa Dahlgren, *New Era*, Apr. 1992, pp. 8-10. The impossible challenge of swimming the distance in three-and-a-half minutes to keep her job became possible.

MORMONADS

"Faith without Works Doesn't Work," *New Era*, July 1991, p. 33. Poster shows a boy in a boat without oars.

"How Do You Punctuate the Gospel?" *New Era*, June 1984, p. 7. Posters shows boys wearing shirts with period, question mark, or exclamation mark, and matching expression.

"Need to Talk? With Prayer You'll Never Get a Busy Signal," *New Era*, June 1985, p. 15. Poster shows telephone in the sky.

"Seek the Best Christmas Presence," *New Era*, Dec. 1991, p. 15. Poster shows a picture of Christ.

Faith

Music Resources

HYMNS AND SONGS FOR YOUNG WOMEN OPENING EXERCISES

"As Zion's Youth" . . . . *Hymns*, no. 256

"How Great Thou Art" . . . . *Hymns*, no. 86

"I Believe in Christ" . . . . *Hymns*, no. 134

"I Know My Father Lives" . . . . *Hymns*, no. 302

"I Know That My Redeemer Lives" . . . . *Hymns*, no. 136

"I Walk by Faith" . . . . *New Era*, Nov. 1985, p. 14

AUDIO TAPES*

Songs	*Albums*
"By the Power of His Word" . . . . *Hold to the Rod 7-12*
"Hear and Hearken" . . . . *Hold to the Rod 7-12*
"Hearts to Understand" . . . . *Hold to the Rod 7-12*
"I Feel the Answer" . . . . *Free to Choose*
"I Walk by Faith" . . . . *Music from Young Women Firesides*
"Listen Well" . . . . *Free to Choose*
"Sharing the Gospel" . . . . *Music for the Young Women Part B*
"Walk His Way" . . . . *Old Testament Media Songs*
"Will He Really Answer Me?" . . . . *Free to Choose*

MUSIC FOR SPECIAL NUMBERS

"A Voice Whispers from the Earth" . . . . *New Era*, Aug. 1991, p. 51

"He Is Our Guide" . . . . *New Era*, Apr. 1991, p. 10

"I Walk by Faith" . . . . *New Era*, Nov. 1985, p. 14

"I Will Come unto Christ" . . . . *New Era*, Apr. 1992, p. 11

"I Will Lead You" . . . . *New Era*, Oct. 1989, p. 24

"Seeds of Truth" . . . . *New Era*, Aug. 1991, p. 10

"Sharing the Gospel" . . . . *A Song of the Heart*, p. 52*

"This Is Jesus" . . . . *New Era*, Apr. 1990, p. 10

"With Heart and Voice" . . . . *New Era*, Apr. 1989, p. 7

---

* Available from Church Distribution. *Free to Choose* and *Hold to the Rod* also available
as songbooks. See page 109 of this book for details.

THE SEED WITHIN YOUR HEART

Brightly ♩=72

Words and Music by Cathy P. Shepherd

Once there was a man sow-ing seeds a-long his way. One fell by the way - side there it lay.
Then there was a seed that was sown on fer-tile ground. It sprang up from good earth it had found.
I will plant a seed, plant the word of God in me. It will grow if I live faith-ful-ly.

One fell on a rock one was blown by winds a-stray, Not one seed would grow, they with-ered all a - way.
It took root and grew grow-ing stron-ger ev'-ry day. Soon it burst with gor-geous flow-ers in ar - ray.
I'll serve and o-bey, hon-or par-ents ev'-ry day, read the scrip-tures, tell the truth, and al-ways pray.

Plant a seed with-in your heart. Watch it grow with faith and love.

Plant a lit-tle seed with-in your heart. Watch it bloom as you serve with love.

Divine Nature

I have inherited divine qualities which I will strive to develop.

"Be partakers of the divine nature, . . . giving all diligence, add to your faith virtue; and to virtue knowledge; And to knowledge temperance; and to temperance patience; and to patience godliness; And to godliness brotherly kindness; and to brotherly kindness charity."

2 Peter 1:4-7

Divine Nature

A Friend Like Jesus

"A friend loveth at all times." Proverbs 17:17

OBJECTIVE:

To help girls develop true friendship and to recognize that friendship is a divine quality that was exemplified by Jesus Christ.

PREPARATION:

Make copies of "Young Women News" (see the following page).

PROCEDURE:

(Choose experiences from this list which meet the needs of your girls.)

• Select *New Era* Q&A articles with the needs of the girls in mind. Use the questions in the articles as an advice column, and read the situations aloud. Have each girl write her answers anonymously on "Young Women News" papers. Collect the answers and read and talk about them. Share a few comments from the *New Era* to reinforce important points.

• Have the girls create and act out role plays so they can practice friendship skills. Situations can be assigned by the advisor in order to meet current needs among the members of the group, or the girls can dramatize situations using their own experiences and imaginations.

• Friendship is divine in nature. Jesus is our great example of friendship. Have the girls tell or read a story showing how Jesus treated his friends. Include John 15:12.

• Discuss the idea that Jesus is a friend to us today. One girl discovered that she "had a friend . . . who would always be there" ("My Friend," Patricia R. Roper, *New Era*, Apr. 1990, p. 9). A *New Era* Q&A article encouraged young people to think of Christ as "Your Friend from Galilee" while they worked to develop friendships (*New Era*, Sept. 1988, p. 18).

• Use John 15:13-15, which shows that Jesus is our friend. Make sure the girls understand the significance of verse 14. This important scripture also shows that we can be friends to Christ. While discussing the idea of developing a friendship with Christ, Malcolm Jeppsen wrote: "Above all, be a friend of the Savior. . . . If you have not done so previously, now is the time to let him know you consider him your true friend and that you will be a true friend of his." ("Who Is a True Friend?" *Ensign,* May 1990, p. 44.)

- Have the girls choose a Personal Progress goal that will help them to implement divine qualities into their friendships.
- Share true stories—perhaps of the girls themselves—of a good friend lifting another by action and example.
- Teach the song, "In the Savior's Shadow," included at the end of this chapter.

SUGGESTED READINGS:

"Don't Let a Flare-up Come Between You" (Mormonad), *New Era,* July 1990, p. 15.

"Hard Look at Myself," Lyn Austin, *Ensign,* Feb. 1990, p. 64.

"I Will Forgive," Darla Swanson, *New Era,* Oct. 1988, p. 11.

"Needs," Derek Cuthbert, *New Era,* Sept. 1987, pp. 49-50.

"Q&A: Friends That Don't Get Along," *New Era,* Apr. 1991, p. 16.

"Q&A: Making Friends," *New Era,* Aug. 1991, p. 16.

"Q&A: What Can I Do to Fit in at Church?" *New Era,* Dec. 1991, pp. 16-19.

"Q&A: I Don't Feel As If I Belong," *New Era,* Sept. 1988, pp. 16-18.

"Small Miracles of Friendship," Patricia Christensen, *New Era,* Jan. 1990, pp. 26-27.

PERSONAL PROGRESS GOALS:

Beehive 1, Divine Nature #3, #4, #5, and #7; Beehive 2, Divine Nature #1; Mia Maid 1, Divine Nature #2 and #7; Mia Maid 2, Divine Nature #3 and #4.

For discussions of family as friends, see Beehive 2, Divine Nature #5, #6, #7, and #8; Mia Maid 1, Divine Nature #3 and #5; Mia Maid 2, Divine Nature #1, #7, and #8.

Young Women News

Dear Young Woman,

Divine Nature

Divine Qualities Game

OBJECTIVE:

To help the girls recognize divine qualities in human nature.

PREPARATION:

- Have a copy shop copy the game board on 11" x 17" pink card stock (a heavy weight paper). The game board is on two pages that fit together.
- Have a copy shop copy the game cards on 8½" x 11" card stock. (See directions below.)
- Bring one marker for each girl, one die, and a 60-second timer.

MAKING THE GAME CARDS:

1. Make one copy of each page of game cards (see pages 18-20). Cut in half (along the dotted line) the page that lists both talents and historical heroes. These are your master pages.
2. Copy the page of Divine Qualities (such as Stalwart) twice—once on yellow card stock for Storytelling cards and once on blue card stock for Sing-a-Song cards.
3. Copy the half page of Talents (such as Musician) on red card stock.
4. Copy the half page of Historical Heroes (such as Abraham Lincoln) on green card stock.
5. Copy the page of Factual Folks (such as "Name a quality you admire in the person on your right") on purple card stock.
6. Cut the cards apart using a paper cutter.

PROCEDURE:

1. Roll the die to move. Moves can be made in any direction, except diagonally. Players must go around the heart obstacles. More than one player may be on a square at a time.

2. Players must go to a Card Stop, such as Sing-a Song, before trying to earn a card. They may go to the Card Stops in any order. An exact roll of the die is not necessary to land on a Card Stop. Rules for collecting the cards are as follows:

   * Sing-a-Song Stop—The player has sixty seconds to sing at least five words of a song that exemplifies the divine quality on the card.

   * Storytelling Stop—The player has sixty seconds to tell or make up a story that exemplifies the divine quality on the card.

   * Talent Stop—The player performs a charade depicting the talent on the card. The other players have sixty seconds to correctly identify the talent.

   * Historical Heroes Stop—The player describes the historical hero on the card without using the listed characteristic. The other players must guess the identity of the hero and the characteristic within sixty seconds.

   * Factual Folks Stop—After reading the card aloud, the player has sixty seconds to follow the directions.

3. When a player wins a card, her turn is over. When a player doesn't win a card, she tries to win a card on her next turn. Players must remain at a given Card Stop until they win a card.

4. Players must collect two Factual Folks cards. However, they must go to at least one other Card Stop before returning for the second Factual Folks card.

5. The first player to collect all six cards (two Factual Folks cards and one each of the other cards) and reach the temple wins the game.

PERSONAL PROGRESS GOAL:

After they play the game, ask the girls to choose a Divine Nature goal that will help them recognize divine qualities in human nature.

Musician	Seamstress	Abraham Lincoln—Honest	Jesus—Forgiving
Banker	Fashion Designer	George Washington—Truthful	Eliza R. Snow—Poetic
Singer	Jazz Dancer	Helen Keller—Persistent	Joseph Smith—Prayerful
Florist	Hair Stylist	William Shakespeare—Creative	Moses—Long-suffering
Softball Player	Artist	Alma the Younger—Repentant	Jesus—Loved Children
Interior Decorator	Actress	Emma Smith—Supportive Wife	Job—Patient
Writer	Computer Specialist	Lucy Mack Smith—Good Mother	Ruth (Bible)—Loyal
Teacher	Photographer	Mary (Mother of Jesus)—Humble	King Solomon—Wise
Mother	Songwriter	Joseph (in Egypt)—Morally Clean	Esther (Bible)—Courageous
Gymnast	Nurse	Mary Fielding Smith—Faithful	Daniel (Bible)—Courageous
Baker	Student	Nephi—Obedient	Albert Einstein—Intelligent

Stalwart	Inquisitive	Self-confident	Compassionate
Cheerful	Loving	Prayerful	Persistent
Friendly	Dependable	Appreciative	Understanding
Kind	Giving	Recognizes Good in Others	Keeps Promises
Loyal	Peacemaker	Serves	Has Faith
Courageous	Honest	Has Integrity	Uses Clean Speech
Thrifty	Humble	Obedient	Morally Clean
Truthful	Creative	Open-minded	Intelligent
Forgiving	Willing to Try	Patient	Inventive
Thoughtful	Has a Sense of Humor	Hopeful	Tenderhearted
Unselfish	Calm	Studious	Gentle

Name a quality you admire in the person on your right.	Identify one talent Heavenly Father gave you.	Name a school teacher you like and explain why.	Name a quality you admire in a young man at school.
Name a quality you admire in the person on your left.	Share something nice that your brother or sister did for you.	Name a Primary teacher you remember and explain why.	Name a talent you admire in a friend from school.
Name a quality you like about yourself.	Name a quality you admire in your advisor.	Tell about something nice that you did for your mother or stepmother.	Tell about something nice that you did for your father or stepfather.
Share something nice that someone in the group did.	Name a good quality of a girl who is absent.	Name a quality you admire in your mother or stepmother.	Name a career in which you could use your talents.
Share something special that your mom or dad did for you.	Share a compliment you gave someone else.	Name a quality you admire in your father or stepfather.	Name a person you admire for his or her cheerfulness.
Name a good quality of your brother or sister.	Share a compliment someone gave you recently.	Name one talent you would like to develop.	Name a person who is a good example to you.
Name a Christlike quality of your bishop.	Name a Christlike quality of the President of the Church.	Name a quality you admire in one of your grandparents.	Name a girl you admire for her strong testimony.
State one reason why you like your best friend.	Name a good quality of your Young Women president.	Tell about a neighbor's good deed.	Name a General Authority you admire and explain why.
Name a quality you like in the person opposite you.	Name a woman in the ward you admire and explain why.	Name a good quality of the Young Men president.	Share something you learned from working on a Personal Progress goal.
Name a characteristic you inherited from your mom.	Name a man in your ward you admire and explain why.	Name a quality you admire in a young man in your ward.	Name something you did recently that made you feel good.

DIVINE QUALITIES GAME

START

START

SING-A-SONG

BLUE CARDS

CARD STOP

START

START

GREEN CARDS

HISTORICAL HEROES

CARD STOP

FACTUAL FOLKS

PURPLE CARDS

START

START

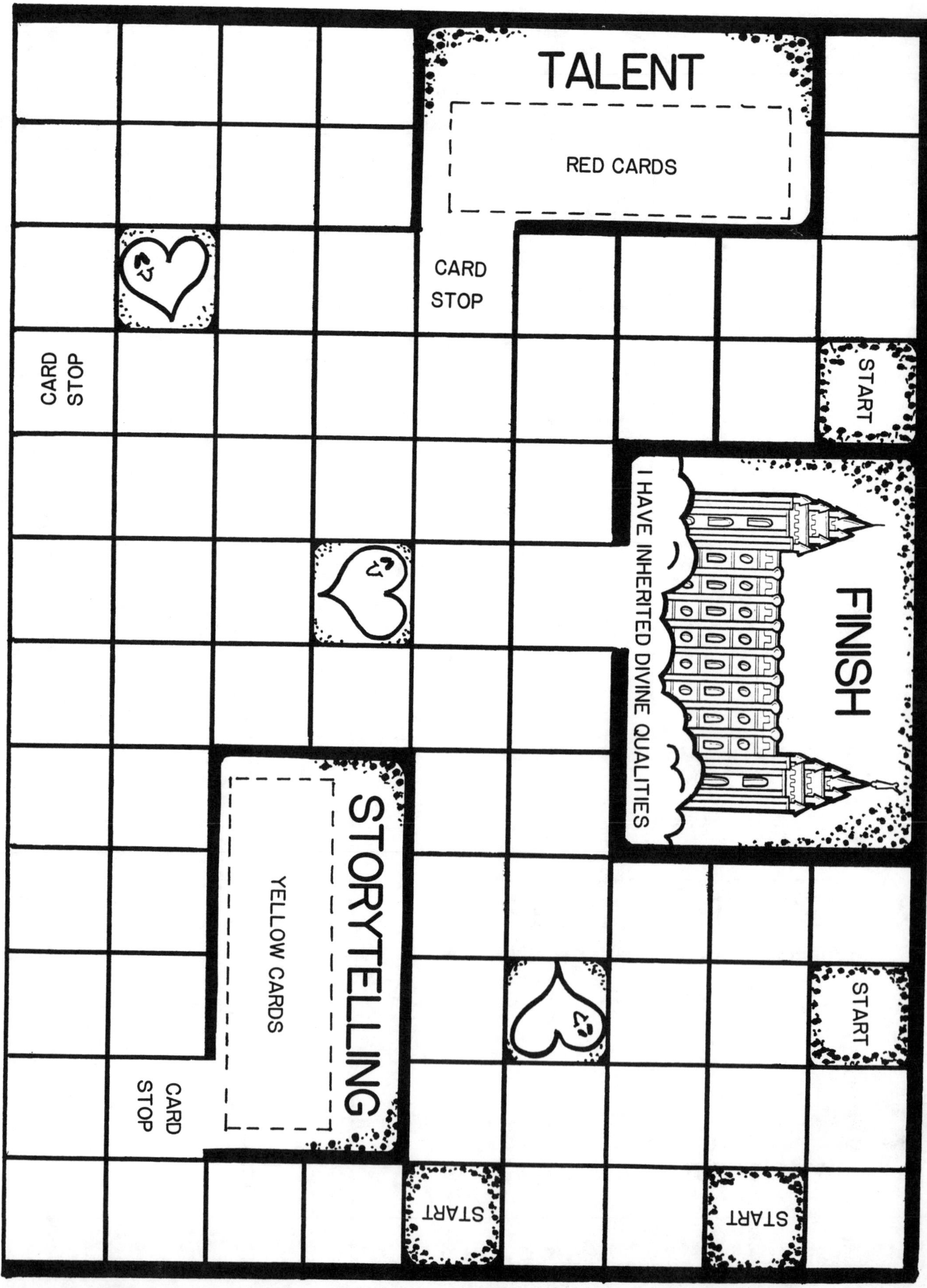

TALENT

RED CARDS

CARD STOP

CARD STOP

START

I HAVE INHERITED DIVINE QUALITIES

FINISH

STORYTELLING

YELLOW CARDS

CARD STOP

START

START

START

Divine Nature

Family Relationships

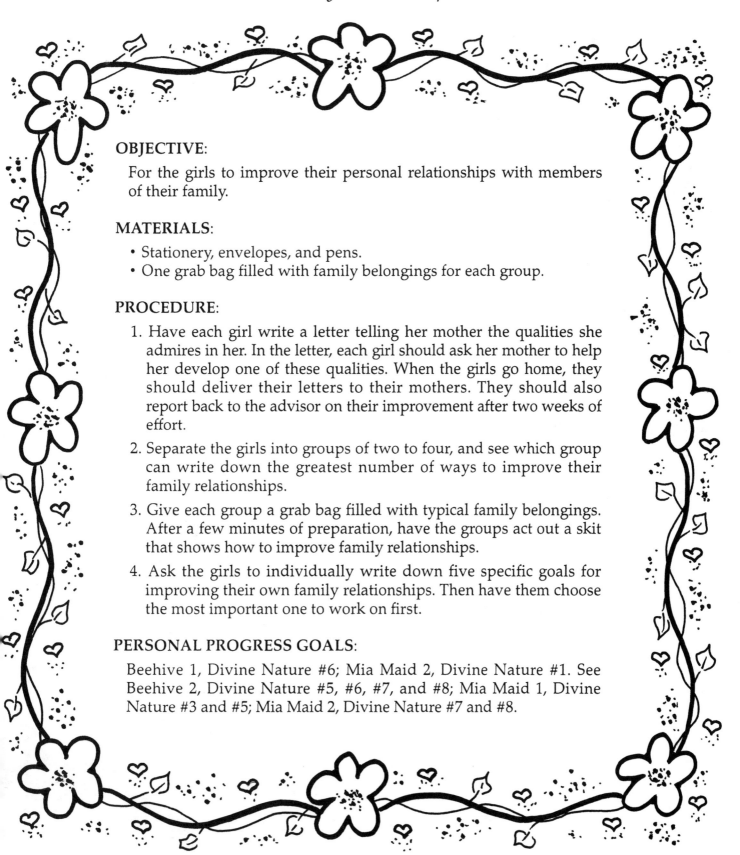

OBJECTIVE:

For the girls to improve their personal relationships with members of their family.

MATERIALS:

- Stationery, envelopes, and pens.
- One grab bag filled with family belongings for each group.

PROCEDURE:

1. Have each girl write a letter telling her mother the qualities she admires in her. In the letter, each girl should ask her mother to help her develop one of these qualities. When the girls go home, they should deliver their letters to their mothers. They should also report back to the advisor on their improvement after two weeks of effort.

2. Separate the girls into groups of two to four, and see which group can write down the greatest number of ways to improve their family relationships.

3. Give each group a grab bag filled with typical family belongings. After a few minutes of preparation, have the groups act out a skit that shows how to improve family relationships.

4. Ask the girls to individually write down five specific goals for improving their own family relationships. Then have them choose the most important one to work on first.

PERSONAL PROGRESS GOALS:

Beehive 1, Divine Nature #6; Mia Maid 2, Divine Nature #1. See Beehive 2, Divine Nature #5, #6, #7, and #8; Mia Maid 1, Divine Nature #3 and #5; Mia Maid 2, Divine Nature #7 and #8.

Divine Nature

Night Compass Course

OBJECTIVE:

To use the beauty of a starry night to help the girls reflect on their divine nature.

PREPARATION:

- Attach each of six bicycle reflectors onto a different tree.
- Photocopy the course directions on the next page and cut them apart. As you set up the course, fill in the blanks and hang one direction by each reflector.
- Assign each girl to bring a flashlight and a compass.
- Bring a treat (optional).

PROCEDURE:

1. This experience works best in a wooded area, away from city lights. In order for it to have a spiritual impact, the girls must be silent except for the one who quietly reads aloud the course directions at each stop. Be sure that the girls know how to use a compass before they begin.

2. Make sure that the course is easy so no one gets lost. The distance between reflectors should be about 100 to 150 feet with no major obstacles in between them.

3. Keep the groups small (four to five girls) and separate them by staggering their starting time. For large groups, set up multiple courses. This allows more girls to have hands-on compass practice. More importantly, keeping the groups small and having the members of each group stay together heightens the girls' sense of intimacy with the Spirit.

EXAMPLE:

This night compass course has been used effectively at stake Young Women camps as a "silent hike." During this activity, the girls not only practiced using a compass and enjoyed the fun of finding the reflectors, but they also pondered on the message of who they are. When this experience was held on a Sunday night, the girls gathered afterwards for a short fireside talk, which compared the gospel to a light and a compass in their lives.

PERSONAL PROGRESS GOAL:

End the experience by having the girls set a Divine Nature Optional Goal that has grown out of the feelings they had during this experience.

COURSE DIRECTIONS

1. (At the starting point)

    Go _____° for _____ feet to the first reflector.

2. (At the first reflector)

    Have you ever had a quiet time when you were able to think about life, look at the stars and our beautiful world, and wonder how you fit into the universe?

    Go _____° for _____ feet to the second reflector.

3. (At the second reflector)

    Who am I? Why am I here? What is the purpose of life? Where am I going?
    It is important to know the answers to these questions. The gospel provides me with answers that give divine direction and purpose to my life.

    Go _____° for _____ feet to the third reflector.

4. (At the third reflector) **Who am I?**

    I am a spirit child of God. He placed me here on earth and gave me a physical body. He loves each person on earth. When I look at the stars twinkling in the beautiful night sky, I remember that he watches over me. I am a daughter of my Heavenly Father, who knows me and tenderly loves me.

    Go _____° for _____ feet to the fourth reflector.

5. (At the fourth reflector) **Why am I here?**

    I came to earth to get a physical body so I can learn to choose the right and to grow and progress. I need to have a guide through life, just like my flashlight and compass, which are leading me now. The "compass" that shows me the direction I should go is the gospel of Jesus Christ. The "flashlight" that helps me see the right path is the Holy Ghost. My spiritual flashlight and compass tell me why I am here. I will have faith in Jesus Christ.

    Go _____° for _____ feet to the fifth reflector.

6. (At the fifth reflector) **What is the purpose of life on earth?**

    In Abraham 3:25 I read that God sent me here to prove me and to see if I will do what he commands. Just as I stumble over rocks and broken branches in the dark, I struggle with obstacles in life. I may stumble or get scratched, but Jesus Christ can heal me. I can safely reach my goals.

    Go _____° for _____ feet to the sixth reflector.

7. (At the sixth reflector) **Where am I going?**

    As I develop my divine qualities and live by the Young Women values, I will prepare to return to my Heavenly Father and to enjoy the blessings of exaltation. The gospel of Jesus Christ offers me lasting joy and helps make my daily life beautiful.

    Go to _____ for a special treat.

Divine Nature

Lesson Resources

ARTICLES

"A Letter-Perfect Christmas," Rebecca Russell, *New Era*, Dec. 1991, p. 29. Seminary students exchanged notes of admiration instead of gifts.

"Better Than Royalty," Elaine Jack, *New Era*, Nov. 1990, pp. 34-37. Our divine heritage includes the Lord's love.

"Be Who You Will Be, But Be Like Christ," John B. Fish, *New Era*, Dec. 1988, pp. 9-11. Your career choice is not as important as becoming Christlike.

"Building Creativity," Dean L. Larsen, *New Era*, Aug. 1991, pp. 4-6. You do have talents, and you can develop and use them.

"Miranda's Magic Box," Brad Wilcox, *New Era*, Sept. 1990, pp. 8-11. Through an enchanting tot, Brad discovered that we brought self-worth with us to this life.

"My Remarkable Brother Eric," Roch S. V. Player, *New Era*, June 1991, pp.12-14. By recognizing her disabled brother's strengths, she changed her own life.

"Q&A: How Can I Control My Anger?" *New Era*, Oct. 1990, pp. 16-19.

"Q&A: How Can I Get My Mouth Under Control?" *New Era*, May 1992, pp. 16-18.

"Rise to the Stature of the Divine within You," Gordon B. Hinckley, *Ensign*, Nov. 1989, pp. 94-98. This article discusses traits such as honor, sensitivity, education, talents, and faith.

"The Magnificence of Man," Russell M. Nelson, *New Era*, Oct. 1987, pp. 44-50. Our magnificence is our divine inheritance.

"The Snob," Cheryl J. Preece, *New Era*, Feb. 1992, pp. 8-11. The "snob" teaches us a powerful lesson in accepting others.

MORMONADS

"Begin to Let Grow," *New Era*, Aug. 1991, p. 7. "Nurture your creative nature. After all, you take after your Father and He was the ultimate Creator."

"Go the Extra Smile," *New Era*, Sept. 1986, p. 19. The poster shows a girl being kind to a little sister who got into her makeup.

"Make Your Appeal More Than Skin Deep," *New Era*, Mar. 1992, p. 37. Poster shows a pickle in a banana peel.

"There Aren't Any Frogs—Just Handsome Princes Who Don't Know Who They Are," *New Era*, Sept. 1988, p. 19. The poster shows a frog on lily pad in front of a castle.

"You Can Conquer Giant Problems," *New Era*, Mar. 1990, p. 9. The poster shows a modern "David" leaning against a sandaled foot that is nearly as tall as he is.

POETRY

"Fathers," Rachel Kellum, *New Era*, Aug. 1989, p. 29. Her father asked, "Are you trying to see the face your Heavenly Father sees?"

Divine Nature

Music Resources

HYMNS AND SONGS FOR YOUNG WOMEN OPENING EXERCISES

"Children of Our Heavenly Father" ....*Hymns*, no. 299
"Dearest Children, God Is Near You" ....*Hymns*, no. 96
"Families Can Be Together Forever" ....*Hymns*, no. 300
"I Am a Child of God" ....*Hymns*, no. 301
"O My Father" ....*Hymns*, no. 292
"Oh, What Songs of the Heart" ....*Hymns*, no. 286

AUDIO TAPES*

Songs   *Albums*

"A Daughter of My Heavenly Father" ....*Music for the Young Women Part B*
"Circle of Friendship" ....*Music for the Young Women Part A*
"Gently" ....*Music for the Young Women Part A*
"Our Father's Plan" ....*Old Testament Media Songs*

MUSIC FOR SPECIAL NUMBERS

"A Daughter of My Heavenly Father" ....*A Song of the Heart*, p. 38*
"Circle of Friendship" ....*A Song of the Heart*, p. 30
"Gently" ....*A Song of the Heart*, p. 58
"I Am a Daughter of God" ....*New Era*, Mar. 1992, p. 10
"We Are Your Daughters" ....*New Era*, Aug. 1989, p. 10

---

*Available from Church Distribution. See page 109 of this book for details.

IN THE SAVIOR'S SHADOW

Words and Music by Barbara G. Dykstra
Arr. Laurie T. Howell

With Emotion

29

grate - ful my friend, for love that grows with ev' - ry

day. For you and for him your earth-ly paths show me the

way. He said from the start our

friend he would be. Let's be friends for - ev - er through

all e - ter - ni - ty. Rit.

Individual Worth

I am of infinite worth with my own divine mission which I will strive to fulfill.

"Remember the worth of souls is great in the sight of God."

D&C : 18:10

Individual Worth

Charlotte's Web Activity

OBJECTIVES:

To increase each young woman's positive feelings about herself and to create unity among the girls.

MATERIALS:

- Paper and pen for each girl.
- Copies of the spider web (see page 34).
- The book *I Walk by Faith,* by Ardeth Greene Kapp (optional).
- The book *Charlotte's Web,* by E. B. White and/or the video *Charlotte's Web* (94 min.) (optional).

PROCEDURE:

1. Determine ahead of time whether the girls are familiar with *Charlotte's Web*. You may want to start spinning the magic of the evening by reading excerpts from the book or showing part of the video. Briefly discuss with the girls ways to overcome a "Wilbur day." Lead into the discussion with this quote by Ardeth Greene Kapp:

Poor Wilbur had some very hard times and often felt alone and discouraged. On one dreary rainy day, we read, he felt so "friendless, dejected, and hungry, he threw himself down in the manure and sobbed."

Have you ever had a Wilbur day? A day when you felt that alone and discouraged? Let me remind you of how Wilbur was rescued from his sad plight. He was visited by his dear friend Charlotte, the spider whom he didn't like at all when he first met her. But over the years he discovered a true friend in Charlotte, one who was willing to save his life by tirelessly spinning a beautiful web with a message that would let people know he was no ordinary pig. Even Wilbur began to believe he was something special because his friend told him he was. (*I Walk by Faith*, p. 139.)

Wilbur is touched by Charlotte's efforts for him and tries to protest that he does not deserve such kind treatment. In response, Charlotte replies, "You have been my friend. That in itself is a tremendous thing. I wove my webs for you because I liked you." (*Ibid.*, p. 140.)

2. Let the girls help create a "web" for each other. Distribute paper and pens. Each girl puts her name at the top of a piece of paper and passes it to the girl on her right. The second girl writes a brief positive statement about the girl whose name is at the top of the paper. They pass the papers around until every girl has written uplifting comments about every other girl. At the end of the activity, each girl will have a "web" to take home. When she has those "friendless, lonesome, and discouraging" days, she can look at her "web" and be rescued.

SUGGESTIONS:

Give each girl a photocopy of the "spider web" (found on the next page) to write on. If you create this experience in October, use spooky spiders and fake webs as decorations. If you want refreshments, decorate a sheet cake with a frosting web and a plastic spider to compliment the theme.

PERSONAL PROGRESS GOALS:

Mia Maid 1, Individual Worth #4; Mia Maid 2, Individual Worth #3.

I'm no ordinary girl!

Individual Worth

Getting-to-Know-You Trivia Game

OBJECTIVES:

To include and involve new and less active girls in an enjoyable, comfortable activity and to help all the girls get to know one another better.

PREPARATION:

- Arrange for transportation and a home to meet in.
- Bring index cards and pens.
- Arrange for munchies.

? ? ? ? ? ? ? ? ? ?

WHO'S WHO IN YOUNG WOMEN?

Come to our activity and find out some interesting facts!

DATE: TIME:

PLACE:

? ? ? ? ? ? ? ? ? ? ?

PROCEDURE:

After you have arranged for a home, "kidnap" the girls your class wants to make an effort to include and take them there on the night you have planned this activity. Divide the girls into two teams and give each girl ten index cards on which to write something about herself. Combine all the cards for each team and mix them up. The leader reads aloud the facts from the cards so the girls can't identify one another by their handwriting. The teams take turns guessing who wrote each card. Let the girls eat munchies during the trivia game.

COMMENTS:

You will learn some interesting facts—everything from "I like (boy's name)" to "My grandma spent a night in the county jail." The objective is met in a fun way.

PERSONAL PROGRESS GOALS:

Encourage the girls to set an Individual Worth Optional Goal to be friendly in specific ways to the girls who were "kidnapped." See Mia Maid 1, Individual Worth #9.

Individual Worth

Individual Worth Cookies

OBJECTIVES:

To include the less active girls and to help each girl see her individual importance.

PREPARATION:

- Assign each girl to bring one ingredient for making cookies.
- Arrange for a kitchen and needed utensils.
- Bring good homemade cookies for backup refreshments.
- Assign the girls to bring their Personal Progress books.

PROCEDURE:

Use a cookie recipe that will fail if any ingredient is missing. If there are too few ingredients to assign one to each girl, divide in half the measured amount of each ingredient called for and assign the girls to bring those partial amounts. If any ingredient is missing because a girl forgot to bring it or because someone did not attend, make the dough without it. The disagreeable taste of the cookies will show that each girl is an important part of the group. If everyone follows through and the cookies taste great, compliment the girls. Their success was made possible by the combined efforts of each individual.

PERSONAL PROGRESS GOALS:

Beehive 1, Faith #8; Mia Maid 1, Faith #2. While the cookies are baking, the girls can set and/or sign off goals.

SOMETHIN'S COOKIN'!

Come find out what it is . . . at Mutual Activity Night!

Date: Time:

Place:

Please bring the following:

_____

Individual Worth

Manicure/Pedicure

OBJECTIVE:

To use a nail care activity to promote individual worth.

PREPARATION:

Ask the girls to bring their own nail care supplies to share.

PROCEDURE:

Let the girls give each other manicures and/or pedicures.

EXAMPLE:

One Mia Maid class discovered that caring for one another's feet was an especially intimate sharing time. The leader compared the one-on-one service to the personal care Jesus gave his disciples when he washed their feet. This activity was a unique way of fostering feelings of worth among the girls in the class. They loved it.

ONE, TWO—
It's just for you!
THREE, FOUR—
Come find out more!
FIVE, SIX—
Pretty nails we'll fix!
SEVEN, EIGHT—
So don't be late!

Date:

Time:

Place:

RECOMMENDED MATERIALS:

- Basin of water with soap and towel.
- Library picture OQ 168, *Anointing of Jesus' Feet*.
- Library picture OQ 550, *Jesus Washing the Disciples' Feet*. Or Mormonad, "He That Is Greatest among You Shall Be Your Servant," which shows Christ washing the disciples' feet (*New Era*, Mar. 1988, p. 27).

SUGGESTIONS:

To heighten the spirituality of the activity, read the scriptural accounts of Mary anointing Jesus (John 12:3), a woman anointing Jesus (Matthew 26:7-13; Mark 14:3-9; Luke 7:37-50), and Jesus washing the disciples' feet (John 13:2-5).

PERSONAL PROGRESS GOAL:

See Mia Maid 1, Individual Worth #9.

Individual Worth

Worth of a Widow

OBJECTIVE:

To help girls appreciate the worth of elderly people.

PROCEDURE:

Arrange a visit with an elderly person in the area.

EXAMPLE:

A Beehive II class visited a nonmember woman who lived near the church. She was an 83-year-old widow. They asked her in advance to share stories about her life while she was growing up in their town. When they went to visit her, she played old-fashioned games with them. She then proceeded to fascinate them for an hour by telling them about local pioneer life. They recorded her stories on cassette tape. The advisor later transcribed these stories and gave them to the woman for Christmas. Since she had never written her own life history, the woman and her family cherish this record.

SUGGESTED READING:

"If Anybody Wants to Listen," Virginia H. Rollings, *New Era,* July 1988, pp. 36-39.

SUGGESTION:

Use the experience to help the girls realize the value of keeping journals. Give them a copy of the following page and allow them time to write down and preserve their feelings about this activity.

PERSONAL PROGRESS GOAL:

Keeping a journal is one of the girls' Personal Progress goals each year.

Jot this down...

Games to play and stories to hear, By someone we think is very dear.

Date: **Time:**
Place:

Bring your pencils - you'll want to write about this evening!

Date _____

Tonight we had a special Young Women activity. These are my thoughts:

_____

_____

_____

_____

_____

_____

_____

_____

_____

_____

_____

_____

_____

_____

_____

_____

_____

Individual Worth

Lesson Resources

ARTICLES

"Chickens, Junkyards, and Carnival People," Greg Jensen, *New Era*, Jan. 1989, pp. 30-33. Be kind to those who are different.

"Dogs Can't Fly," Ron Sellstern, *New Era*, June 1990, pp. 44-47. Do we, like the dogs with the fence removed, hold *ourselves* back?

"Everyone Belongs," A. Lynn Scoresby, *New Era*, Oct. 1987, pp. 8-11. A tragedy forces the high school students to work at including everyone.

"Identity of a Young Woman," Elaine L. Jack, *Ensign*, Nov. 1989, pp. 86-88. Article includes examples from girls that show their divine nature and worth.

"I'm Sorry, Bertha," Sheron S. Gibb, *New Era*, Sept. 1989, pp. 44-46. She asks herself the question, "How could I have treated her like that?"

"Q&A: How Can I Feel Good on the Inside When I'm Ugly on the Outside?" *New Era*, June 1992, pp. 16-18.

"Q&A: How Can I Change Low Self-Esteem?" *New Era*, Mar. 1990, pp. 16-19.

"Self-Worth," (FYI), *New Era*, May 1991, p. 40. Accompanying photograph shows a youth seeing himself in a distorted mirror.

"The Mystery in Your Homeroom," Jeanne-Marie Bell, *New Era*, Oct. 1987, pp. 26-28. Detect an interesting person hiding behind shyness.

"The Name Game," Geri Christensen, *New Era*, Mar. 1991, pp. 48-50. Just learning everyone's names made a big difference in how Geri felt about herself.

"The Only One in Step," David Hugh Birley, *New Era*, May 1979, pp. 34-36. One bass drummer insisted he was right when everyone else was wrong.

"Who Do We Think We Are?" Jean S. Marshall, *New Era*, Feb. 1988, pp. 12-14. Three short examples taught Jean to see the worth of others.

"Voices of Spring," Layne H. Dearden, *New Era*, June 1988, pp. 48-50. A rattlesnake taught the powerful lesson that God knew who Layne was.

"Why Not Beautiful?" Diane L. Mangum, *New Era*, Nov. 1991, p. 26. A plain girl realizes that, like Esther, she may have something to accomplish.

"Woman—of Infinite Worth," Russell M. Nelson, *Ensign*, Nov. 1989, pp. 20-22. The article quotes and expands on this Young Women value.

MORMONADS

"Differences Can Be Appealing," *New Era*, Feb. 1990, p. 7. Poster shows apple, orange, and banana separately and as a fruit salad.

"Don't Limit Yourself," *New Era*, May 1990, p. 15. Poster shows boy boxed in with a fence that says, "I can't."

"We Can All Be Winners," *New Era*, July 1984, p. 7. Poster shows youth on risers with Olympic ribbons.

"You Don't Have to Be a Big Wheel," *New Era*, Mar. 1986, p. 7. Poster shows a little gear turning big ones.

Individual Worth

Music Resources

HYMNS AND SONGS FOR YOUNG WOMEN OPENING EXERCISES

"Dear to the Heart of the Shepherd" . . . . *Hymns*, no. 221

"God Loved Us, So He Sent His Son" . . . . *Hymns*, no. 187

"I Stand All Amazed" . . . . *Hymns*, no. 193

"Whenever I Hear the Song of a Bird" . . . . *Children's Songbook*, p. 228*

AUDIO TAPES*

Songs	Albums
"A Family Is Forever"	*Music for the Young Women Part A*
"Do You Know I'm Here?"	*Music for the Young Women Part A*
"I'll Be All I Can"	*Old Testament Media Songs*
"The Worth of Souls"	*Hold to the Rod 1-6* (instrumental)
"Today Is My Day"	*Music for the Young Women Part B*
"When Someone Cares"	*Music for the Young Women Part A*

MUSIC FOR SPECIAL NUMBERS

"A Family Is Forever" . . . . *A Song of the Heart*, p. 28

"Do You Know I'm Here?" . . . . *A Song of the Heart*, p. 79

"Today Is My Day" . . . . *A Song of the Heart*, p. 35

"When Someone Cares" . . . . *A Song of the Heart*, p. 1

"Come, Hold Your Torches High" . . . . Sheet music*

---

* Available from Church Distribution. See page 109 in this book for details.

I AM A PRINCESS

Majestic

Words and Music by Jodi Johnston

I am a prin - cess. The daugh - ter _____ of the most

lov - ing King. He is my Fa - ther, He

loves me _____ much more than an - y - thing _____ I'll learn to

To Coda ⊕

know Him, to love Him ___ and I will be His daugh - ter ____ I have a
A
To Coda ⊕

mis - sion a pur - pose ___ that I will strive to ful -

fill. _____ I need great faith _____ in His plan. I must be - lieve _____ in
grow _____ and choose right, I'll do good works _____ for

43

His Son,   I am di-vine;   I have great worth.
oth-ers.   In-teg-ri-ty,   I will be true.

I am His child, _____ so I will fill _____ my mis-sion here. ____ I'll learn to

here. ___   I am a prin-cess ___ I have a mis-sion   I

Rit. will   ful - fill.

Knowledge

I will continually seek opportunities for learning and growth.

"Seek learning, even by study and also by faith."

D&C 88:118

Knowledge

Get Ready, Get Set . . .

OBJECTIVES:

To acquaint girls with different career choices and to encourage them to prepare for a career.

PREPARATION:

Invite women from a variety of vocational backgrounds, including an exemplary mother, to serve on a panel.

PROCEDURE:

Have each panelist present a practical, realistic overview of her profession. Panelists should stress the importance of preparation and that, while in their youth, the girls should "get ready" and "get set" so they can "go" into satisfying careers as adults. Panelists should also discuss the spiritual ramifications of their specific career choices, such as the ease or difficulty they have fulfilling family responsibilities while they are working. Allow the girls time to ask questions.

SUGGESTION:

Involve the girls in choosing which careers are represented.

PERSONAL PROGRESS GOALS:

Mia Maid 1, Knowledge #9; Mia Maid 2, Knowledge #4.

Knowledge

Girls' Basketball Night

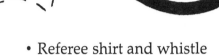

OBJECTIVE:

To activate Young Women of all ages.

PREPARATION:

Arrange for a woman to coach and referee.

MATERIALS:

- Four women's regulation size basketballs
- Two sets of matching colored shirts
- Score book
- Referee shirt and whistle
- Scoreboard equipment

PROCEDURE:

1. Begin with some warm-up drills. This will give the girls more confidence in handling the ball. As a result, more of them will participate and they will play better once the game starts.

2. Let the girls choose teams. A standard team consists of five girls, but groups of any size can play and have fun. Those who do not want to play can cheer.

3. Play a regulation high school girls' game with eight-minute quarters. Hold two, untimed breaks between quarters and a fifteen-minute halftime.

WARM-UP DRILLS:

1. *Zigzag passing.* Separate the girls into two groups. Each group divides into two lines that face each other. Each player throws a chest pass to the person across from her. The last person throws the ball back to the girl she received from to reverse the direction, so the ball goes down the line and back. The two groups race to finish first. Repeat the process with two balls.

2. *Lay-ups.* The girls stand in two lines facing the basket. Each girl in the right line dribbles in and shoots. Each girl in the left line rebounds and passes to the first girl on her right. The first player in each line returns to the end of the other line. Repeat the drill so that the girls in the right line dribble and pass to the girls on the left. The girls on the left then shoot.

3. *Dribbling.* Divide the girls into the same number of lines as there are balls. Players dribble the full length of the court around chairs using their right hands as they go up the court and their left hands as they return. Then they pass to the next person in line.

EXAMPLE:

The girls in one ward insisted that men not coach or referee and that boys not be allowed to watch. They had so much fun that they begged for a repeat of the activity later on. Two girls who refused to come to any other activity came to both games.

PERSONAL PROGRESS GOALS:

Beehive 1, Knowledge #4; Beehive 2, Knowledge #5.

Knowledge
Guitar

OBJECTIVE:

To encourage the girls to develop a new talent.

PREPARATION:

- Arrange for a guitar for each girl.
- Invite a specialist who can teach guitar.
- Make copies of the chords and the song on this page.

PROCEDURE:

Have the specialist teach the girls three simple chords (A, E, D) so they can learn to play "Edelweiss," a song played using only these chords.

EXAMPLE:

One Mia Maid class especially looked forward to guitar night. Excited about their musical adventure, they hurried home from Mutual to practice on their own.

PERSONAL PROGRESS GOALS:

Mia Maid 1, Knowledge #1; Mia Maid 2, Knowledge #1. Or use as an optional goal for Knowledge.

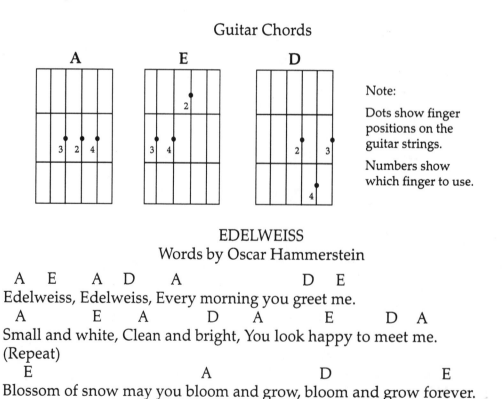

Guitar Chords

Note:

Dots show finger positions on the guitar strings.

Numbers show which finger to use.

EDELWEISS
Words by Oscar Hammerstein

   A   E   A   D   A   D   E
Edelweiss, Edelweiss, Every morning you greet me.

   A   E   A   D   A   E   D A
Small and white, Clean and bright, You look happy to meet me.
(Repeat)

    E   A   D   E
Blossom of snow may you bloom and grow, bloom and grow forever.

   A   E   A   D   A   E   D A
Edelweiss, Edelweiss, Bless my homeland forever.

Knowledge

"This Old Rag" Brag Night

OBJECTIVES:

To teach budgeting, the use of clothing styles, clothing coordination, modesty, grooming, posture, and poise.

PREPARATION:

- Assign the girls to bring clothes that cost less than $10 for the fashion show.
- Assign the girls to bring clothes they do not want or wear anymore.

PROCEDURE:

1. Invite a specialist who can show the girls how to work wardrobe wonders while pinching pennies.
2. Demonstrate posture and modeling techniques for a fashionable flair.
3. End with a fashion show in which the girls model the clothes they bought for $10 or less.
4. Set up a "Rag Grab" table so the girls can donate clothes they no longer want or wear. Anyone is free to take home "new" clothes from this table. Any remaining clothes can be donated to a thrift store.

SUGGESTED STORY:

"The reporter found Cadillacs parked in front of the Salvation Army: Rich people shopping in thrift shops! Well, who didn't know that? Some rich people like a bargain as much as anybody. . . . One attraction: You can find things at thrift shops that you won't find anywhere else. . . . Rich people and poor people and thrifty people and treasure hunters and bargain hunters [are] all drawn to thrift shops." ("Thrift Stores Attract Even the Rich," UPS story from Philadelphia, May 17, 1991.)

PERSONAL PROGRESS GOALS:

Mia Maid 1 and 2, Knowledge #1.

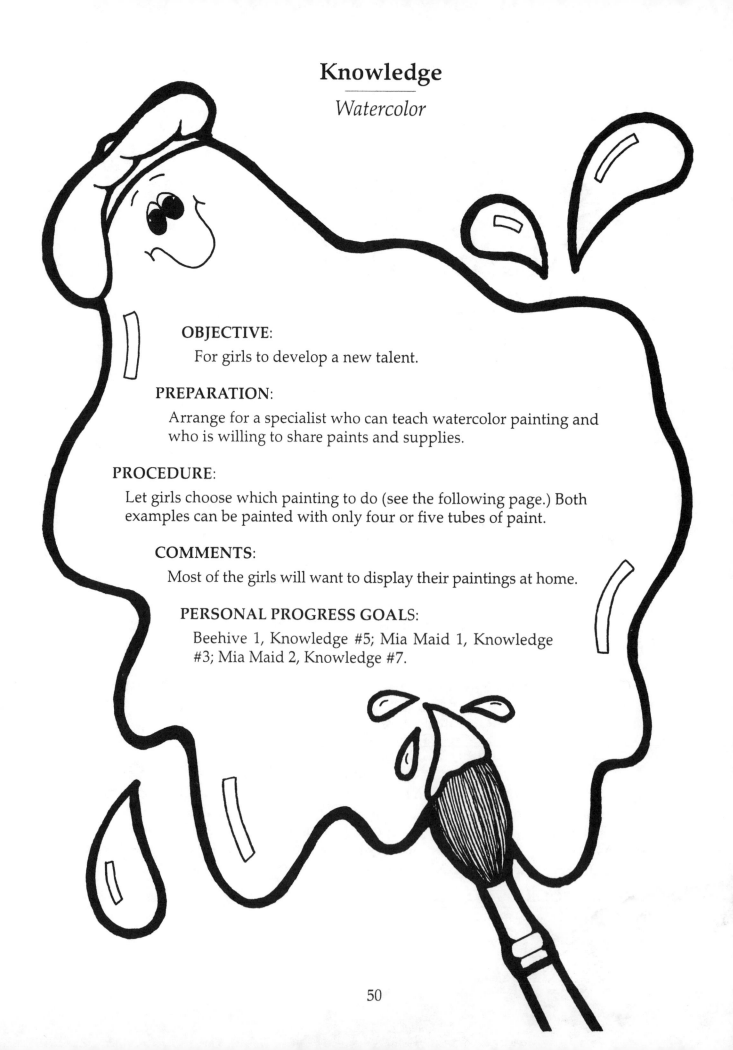

Knowledge

Watercolor

OBJECTIVE:

For girls to develop a new talent.

PREPARATION:

Arrange for a specialist who can teach watercolor painting and who is willing to share paints and supplies.

PROCEDURE:

Let girls choose which painting to do (see the following page.) Both examples can be painted with only four or five tubes of paint.

COMMENTS:

Most of the girls will want to display their paintings at home.

PERSONAL PROGRESS GOALS:

Beehive 1, Knowledge #5; Mia Maid 1, Knowledge #3; Mia Maid 2, Knowledge #7.

Knowledge

Lesson Resources

ARTICLES

"Catching Your Second Wind," Robert K. Thomas, *New Era*, Aug. 1988, pp. 16-19. Being able to read well opens new adventures and the scriptures.

"Do What They Think You Can't Do," Henry B. Eyring, *New Era*, Oct. 1989, pp. 4-6. This article discusses three keys to learning.

"Giving It a College Try," Janet Thomas, *New Era*, Oct. 1991, pp. 44-48. Your success in college starts in high school.

"Good Jellyroll, Fauna," Larry Hiller and B. Kent Harrison, *New Era*, Jan. 1990, pp. 34-38. The importance of math is shown in a humorous way.

"Happily Ever After?" Linda P. Christensen, *New Era*, Jan.-Feb. 1985, pp. 36-40. What will you do if dreams of marriage fall through? Special issue on careers.

"Q&A: How Do I Decide on a Career?" *New Era*, Feb. 1992, p. 16.

"Q&A: Why Shouldn't I Just Drop Out [of School]?" *New Era*, Sept. 1990, pp. 16-19.

"Taking an Essay Test," (FYI), *New Era*, Mar. 1989, p. 40. This article discusses seven tips for success.

"Ten Steps for Easier Studying," *New Era*, Sept. 1984, pp. 35-37. Studying is not a talent; it is a skill you can learn.

"The Discovery," Richard M. Romney, *New Era*, Oct. 1988, pp. 20-26. Choosing a career includes knowing who you want to be.

"The Etiquette Quiz," Diane Lofgren Mangum, *New Era*, Apr. 1989, pp. 12-15. Questions and answers check your knowledge of manners.

"The Magic Five Minutes," Paula Hope Miller, *New Era*, Oct. 1987, pp. 30-31. Implement a quick plan to improve your grades.

FICTION

"Miss Whitney's B," Alma J. Yates, *New Era*, Sept. 1987, pp. 34-39. Challenged to produce his best, Michael started studying to learn.

MORMONADS

"Don't Bail Out," *New Era*, Sept. 1991, p. 15. Let education help move you to a higher "plane." Poster shows parachutist standing on student school desk.

"Read the Instructions," *New Era*, Mar. 1991, p. 15. Poster shows scriptures along with tools and repair instructions.

"Sign of the Times," *New Era*, May 1987, p. 7. Poster shows scriptures in backpack.

"You Can Take It with You," *New Era*, Sept. 1984, p. 7. Poster shows suitcase full of school books and scriptures (quotes D&C 130:18-19.)

Knowledge

Music Resources

HYMNS AND SONGS FOR YOUNG WOMEN OPENING EXERCISES

"As I Search the Holy Scriptures" . . . . *Hymns,* no. 277
"Oh, Holy Words of Truth and Love" . . . . *Hymns,* no. 271
"Oh Say, What Is Truth?" . . . . *Hymns,* no. 272
"Teach Me to Walk in the Light" . . . . *Hymns,* no. 304
"Thy Holy Word" . . . . *Hymns,* no. 279
"Truth Eternal" . . . . *Hymns,* no. 4

SEEK KNOWLEDGE

D&C 88:78-80, 118

Words and Music by Gayla Wise

1. You can take knowl-edge___ with you, The facts and fig - ures___
know the scrip-tures___ tell us Seek learn - ing of all___

learned. So think what real - ly___ mat - ters When your de - gree you've___ earned. What
things In heav - en and in___ earth Of coun - tries and of___ kings. To

does it pro - fit___ you ———— To gain an earth - ly___ goal If in your dai - ly___
mag - ni - fy your___ mission, your - self you must pre - pare. By stu - dy and by___

1.
choic - es___ you al - so lose your soul.
faith___ Gain

2. We wis-dom you can share. You

can take knowl - edge___ with you Of all you've learned since birth.

Seek knowl - edge ev - er learn - ing, For de - grees in heav - en and earth.

Choice and Accountability

I will remain free by choosing good over evil and will accept responsibility for my choices.

"Choose you this day whom ye will serve; . . . but as for me and my house, we will serve the Lord."

Joshua 24:15

Choice and Accountability

Choice and Accountability Treasure Hunt

OBJECTIVES:

To help the girls realize that their personal values determine their daily decisions.

PREPARATION:

- Photocopy the invitation on page 61. Assign each girl to bring a flashlight and a white elephant gift.

- Photocopy the list of 21 value questions found on pages 59-60. Cut these questions apart and tape each one to the outside of an envelope.

- Cut construction paper, in the value colors, into 1½ inch squares. Make six squares of each color per girl.

- In each of the 21 envelopes place the two colors of paper specified by the question on that envelope. Enclose enough squares of each color so each girl can have one. For example, if you have ten girls, in the envelope with question 1, place ten blue squares and ten red squares.

MATERIALS:

- Envelopes. One per girl and 21 additional envelopes for the value choices.
- White, blue, red, green, orange, yellow, and purple construction paper. One sheet each for five girls, or two sheets each for 11 girls.
- Masking tape to hang the envelopes and a pen to write the clues on them.
- Assorted cookies.

SETTING UP THE TREASURE HUNT:

- Set up the treasure hunt by hiding the 21 envelopes on the church grounds and in the parking lot. As you do so, write a simple clue on the outside of each envelope to help the girls find the next envelope. For example, on envelope #1 write, "Find a spotlight in front of the church." Write a clue on envelope #21 that will send the girls to envelope #1.

- Be inventive in hiding the envelopes and in writing the clues for finding them. Some clues should be difficult to follow, and some easy to follow.

- Place the envelopes far enough apart to create a merry chase.
- Put a few envelopes in dark spots so there is a positive consequence for the girls who remember to bring their flashlights and a negative one for those who forget.
- Allow 20 minutes to set up the treasure hunt.

STARTING PROCEDURE:

1. Explain to the girls *what* they are doing, not *why*. Allow them the excitement of "discovery learning."

2. Give each girl an empty envelope. Tell them that, like any other treasure hunt, they will run from clue to clue. However, because this is a Choice and Accountability Treasure Hunt, they will have to make choices at each stop. After making each choice, they will remove from the envelope the colored square that coordinates with their choice and put it into their own envelope.

3. Let the girls group themselves into small teams.

4. To separate the groups, start each one at a different location. For example, if you hide envelopes by the flagpole and the dumpster, send one team to start in each place. They need to follow the clues in order, but they can start anywhere in the sequence. They are finished when they find the clue that sends them to the place where they began.

5. Allow the girls about 20 minutes for the treasure hunt.

ENDING PROCEDURE:

1. Gather the girls to sit on the lawn, in a place where they can see without flashlights, and have them sort their squares into colored piles. Help them realize that the things that are important to them—their values—determined their choices. Let them talk about the decisions they made during the treasure hunt.

2. Make sure they realize that there are no "right" or "wrong" answers to the value choices; both choices are good. Likewise, in life, we must often choose between two good options when making a decision. Nevertheless, we are still accountable for our choices, and we will receive the consequences of these choices.

3. Tell the girls that you intentionally chose 21 clues so that each value could be matched against each of the other values. While each value is illustrated six times, chances are that no one will choose six squares of each color. Lots of squares collected in one value may indicate a personal strength. If any of the girls have a color missing from their envelopes, encourage them to set goals that will help them develop that value.

4. Mention any choices you observed the girls making during the treasure hunt, such as sharing flashlights and helping each other.

5. End the discussion with this question: "The reward given at the end of many treasure hunts is an exciting surprise. Although the surprise cannot be wrapped in a beautiful box, this treasure hunt also has a priceless gift. Have you discovered what it is?" Acceptable answers may vary, but the girls should come to the realization that the opportunities to make choices and to be accountable are indeed priceless gifts from our Heavenly Father.

6. Limit this wrap-up session to about five minutes. Let the activity speak for itself.

EXAMPLE:

Girls in one class made these comments after a treasure hunt: "I've got lots of faith," said one girl. "What value is red?" asked another. "Oh, oh! I don't have any green. Guess that means I don't know very much!" exclaimed a third. The girls had discovered that every choice was related to a value. This activity was a lot of fun for the girls. At the same time, it helped them think about their values and the choices they make.

WHITE ELEPHANT EXCHANGE:

1. Let the first team that finished the treasure hunt choose who starts the white elephant exchange.

2. Tell the girls they may choose from either wrapped or already opened gifts so there are more choices.

3. Afterwards, briefly ask the girls how the white elephant exchange applies to life. For example, ask them how the reactions of the other girls affected their choice and how the choice of each girl affected what the others received.

TREAT:

The girls will quickly realize that since the cookies are varied, they have to make a choice. You want them to choose a treat they like. Point out that in the same way, Heavenly Father wants them to make choices that bring them happiness.

PERSONAL PROGRESS GOALS:

Goals that are suitable for group discussion following the treasure hunt include Beehive 2, Choice and Accountability #3, #4, and #5. Ask the girls to select a Choice and Accountability goal that will help them be accountable for their choices.

Value Choices for Choice and Accountability Treasure Hunt

1. **Which personal progress goal would you be more likely to choose?**

   a. Work to stop criticizing and/or complaining—take blue.
   b. Write a thank-you note to someone who did something for you—take red.

2. **Which personal progress goal would you be more likely to choose?**

   a. Create a poem, story, article, or work of art that illustrates a gospel principle—take green.
   b. Be selective about the TV programs you watch—take orange.

3. **Which personal progress goal would you be more likely to choose?**

   a. Tutor a friend and help her understand her school work—take yellow.
   b. Intentionally be a good influence on your friends—take purple.

4. **Which personal progress goal would you be more likely to choose?**

   a. Bear your testimony—take white.
   b. Talk with your grandparents or an older LDS couple about qualities needed for a successful, happy marriage—take blue.

5. **Which personal progress goal would you be more likely to choose?**

   a. Baby-sit for free—take yellow.
   b. Make friends with someone who needs a friend—take red.

6. **Which personal progress goal would you be more likely to choose?**

   a. Apologize to and do something nice for someone you made unhappy—take orange.
   b. Talk to your mother and one other mother about motherhood—take blue.

7. **Which personal progress goal would you be more likely to choose?**

   a. Learn a new recipe—take green.
   b. Give your honest opinion when someone asks—take purple.

8. **Which personal progress goal would you be more likely to choose?**

   a. Organize a family photo album—take red.
   b. Participate in appropriate Sunday activities—take orange.

9. **Which action would you be more likely to choose?**

   a. Read a *New Era* article—take white.
   b. Watch a TV show on the effects of alcohol—take green.

10. **Which action would you be more likely to choose?**

    a. Help your family when asked even if you don't feel like it—take orange.
    b. Help someone outside your family—take yellow.

11. **Which activity would you be more likely to choose?**

    a. Get to bed on time—take red.
    b. Stay up to finish a book report—take green.

12. **Which action would you be more likely to choose?**

    a. Forgive someone who hurt you—take blue.
    b. Turn down an invitation to a party where a video of questionable content will be shown—take purple.

13. **Which activity would you be more likely to choose?**

    a. Give a family home evening lesson on a family problem—take white.
    b. Give your sister a perm because she thinks her hair is ugly—take red.

14. **Which action would you be more likely to choose?**

    a. Be cheerful even when you don't get your way—take orange.
    b. Buy the more modest dress even though it is more expensive—take purple.

15. **Which activity would you be more likely to choose?**

    a. Read the scriptures for 15 minutes—take white.
    b. Help a brother or a sister with homework—take yellow.

16. **Which would you be more likely to choose?**

    a. Stop an argument—take blue.
    b. Talk to an adult about some question you have—take green.

17. **Which activity would you be more likely to choose?**

    a. Listen to a friend talk about his or her problems—take red.
    b. Clean your room as you promised you would—take purple.

18. **Which activity would you be more likely to choose?**

    a. Learn or create something new for the fun of it—take green.
    b. Write a letter to a missionary or a friend who moved—take yellow.

19. **Which activity would you be more likely to choose?**

    a. Invite a nonmember friend to Sunday meetings—take white.
    b. Do an extra job at home without being asked—take orange.

20. **Which activity would you be more likely to choose?**

    a. Sing an uplifting song to chase away bad thoughts or a bad mood—take blue.
    b. Try to make someone new feel welcome—take yellow.

21. **Which action would you be more likely to choose?**

    a. Admit to your dad or mom that he or she is right—take purple.
    b. Pray for help to get along better with your dad or mom—take white.

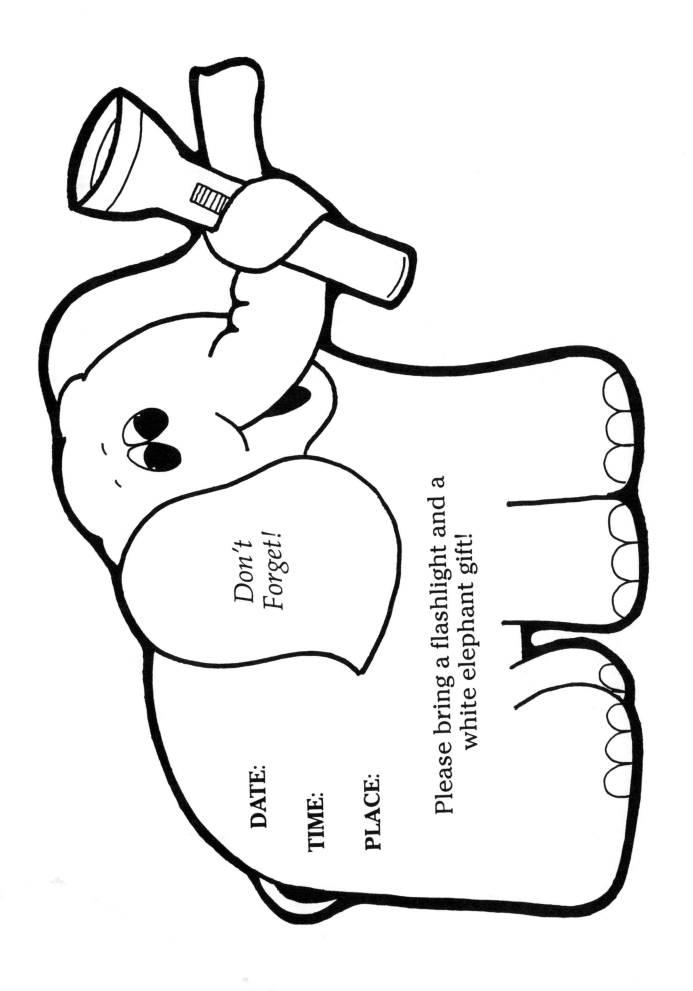

Don't
Forget!

DATE:

TIME:

PLACE:

Please bring a flashlight and a
white elephant gift!

Choice and Accountability

Clothes Shopping Decisions

OBJECTIVES:

To help girls learn to choose modest clothing and to be informed when they make clothing decisions.

PREPARATION:

- Talk to the bishop to discuss safety concerns and to decide on a shopping location. If shopping at a mall is not advisable, stores close to each other will suffice.

- Make a copy of the handout on the following page for each girl.

- Lay the groundwork for the activity ahead of time by having a specialist come in to teach the girls about modesty, fabrics, clothing construction, basic styles versus fads, and colors and lines that flatter each girl personally. They can learn how to build a basic wardrobe to maximize versatility and stretch their clothing dollars.

- When the girls go shopping, ask them to use the concepts that the specialist taught to help them choose three outfits. As a result, they will be prepared to make better decisions when they go clothes shopping on their own.

- Arrange for one adult to accompany each group of 3 or 4 girls to provide safety and supervision when they are shopping. Invite mothers who enjoy camaraderie with their daughters and with youth. This creates an opportunity to foster good mother/daughter relationships, which is one of the goals of the Young Women program.

PROCEDURE:

After arriving at the shopping center, separate the girls into teams. Each team will visit three different stores. Give each girl the handout and a pencil. Although they go as a team, each girl must make her own choices and fill out the handout on her own. Set a time and a place to meet at the end of the activity. Afterwards, let the girls compare their findings. Congratulate them for learning to be careful shoppers.

SUGGESTED READING:

"To Clothe a Temple," John S. Tanner, *Ensign*, Aug. 1992, pp. 44-47.

PERSONAL PROGRESS GOALS:

Beehive 2, Choice and Accountability #2 and #5.

Choosing an Outfit

Instructions:

1. **Window shop for an outfit (dress or skirt and blouse) that is—**
   a. appropriate for church and nice school functions.
   b. washable.
   c. $40 or less.
   d. modest in length (at least to the knees) and has sleeves.
   e. appropriate for the current season.
   f. flattering on you.
   g. traditionally designed so that it won't go out of style quickly.

2. **Go to three different stores and compare outfits chosen according to the characteristics listed above. Complete the following information.**

   Store 1 (name) _____
   Description of outfit: _____
       Style (dress, etc.) _____
       Color _____
       Fabric _____
       Required care _____
       Quality of construction _____
       Cost _____
   What figure flaws does it hide? _____
   What personal strengths does it flatter? _____
   What other pieces of clothing in your wardrobe does it match? _____

   ....

   Store 2 (name) _____
   Description of outfit: _____
       Style (dress, etc.) _____
       Color _____
       Fabric _____
       Required care _____
       Quality of construction _____
       Cost _____
   What figure flaws does it hide? _____
   What personal strengths does it flatter? _____
   What other pieces of clothing in your wardrobe does it match? _____

   ....

   Store 3 (name) _____
   Description of outfit: _____
       Style (dress, etc.) _____
       Color _____
       Fabric _____
       Required care _____
       Quality of construction _____
       Cost _____
   What figure flaws does it hide? _____
   What personal strengths does it flatter? _____
   What other pieces of clothing in your wardrobe does it match? _____

Choice and Accountability

Sewing Simple Dresses

OBJECTIVE:

To encourage each girl to make an item of clothing that reflects Church standards.

PREPARATION:

- Make a dress ahead of time to use as an example.
- Give each girl a pattern two weeks before the activity (see page 66).
- Have the girls buy their own material and thread. To determine the amount of yardage, have the girls measure themselves from the shoulder to the hemline, double that measurement, and add 8". Most girls will need 3 to 3½ yards of fabric, 45" wide.
- Assign the girls to bring scissors, pins, and their previously cut out dress pieces.
- Arrange for one adult leader for every 5 or 6 girls.

Finished Dress
(Wear with a shirt)

MATERIALS:

- Sewing machines—one for every two girls
- Iron and ironing board
- Yarn
- Extension cords

PATTERN:

To enlarge the bodice pattern to actual size, make two photocopies of the pattern at 141% and one photocopy at 120% using 11" x 17" paper. Lengthen the center lines and the side seams according to the size you want (small, medium, or large); draw a bottom edge to connect the center and side. For the small size, lengthen the side seams to 12½", the center front to 15½", and the center back to 19". For the medium size, lengthen the side seams to 12¾", the center front to 16½", and the center back to 20". For the large size, lengthen the side seams to 14½", the center front to 18", and the center back to 21¾".

To cut out the bodice:

Fold the fabric so the selvage edges meet in the center of the folded fabric. Place the center front of the bodice front pattern on one of the folds. Repeat for the bodice back. Pin and cut. Repeat this process so that there are a total of four bodice pieces.

To cut out the skirt:

Measure each girl from the hip to the desired hemline. To this measurement, add 2⅝" for the hem and the seam allowance. Maintain the original width of the fabric (45"), and cut two lengths of fabric using this total measurement.

PROCEDURE: (Make all seams ⅝" deep.)

Bodice:

1. With the right sides together, sew one of the front bodice pieces to one of the back bodice pieces at the side seams, forming a tube. Repeat with the other front and back bodice pieces. Press the seams open.

2. On one of the bodice tubes, fold over the shoulder straps on the ⅝" seam line with the wrong sides together. Press. (See illustration 1.) This piece is the inner bodice.

3. Place the inner bodice inside the other bodice piece with the right sides together. Line up the edges of the fabric at the neckline and the armholes and pin together. Do not pin at the shoulder. Lay the seam allowance of the outer bodice flat at the shoulder. For the inner bodice, make sure the pressed seam allowance is folded over. Pin through the three layers that are made when the fabric is folded over. Sew the armholes from the side edge to the shoulder seam line. Sew the neckline from one shoulder seam line to the other. (See illustration 2.)

4. At ½" intervals, clip through the seam allowance of the armholes and neckline almost to the seam. (See illustration 3.) Turning the fabric right side out and carefully pressing the neckline and armhole seams at this point is important.

5. To join the shoulder seams, on the outer bodice place the material with the right sides together and sew just above the folded inner bodice, making sure that you do not catch the folded edge in the seam. (See illustration 4.)

6. Press the shoulder seams open. Tuck the raw fabric edges inside the folded seam allowance and sew them closed by hand.

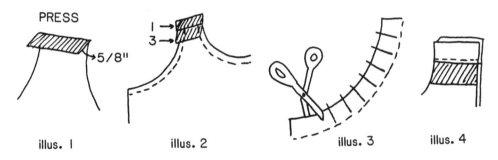

PRESS

→5/8"

illus. 1 illus. 2 illus. 3 illus. 4

Skirt:

1. Sew the side seams together to form a tube. Use a zigzag stitch to sew a length of yarn all the way around the top edge of the skirt. Pull the yarn to gather the skirt.

2. Pin the top of the skirt to the outer bodice with the right sides together; match the side seams. Adjust the gathers so they are evenly distributed around the top of the skirt and sew.

3. To finish the inside of the dress, fold under the seam allowance along the bottom edge of the inner bodice. Pin in place and hand stitch.

4. To hem the skirt, fold the fabric up 1" and press. Repeat. Hem with a topstitch.

VARIATION:

Girls can make their dresses unique by adding a row of buttons down the front, appliques to the bodice, or patch pockets to the skirt. Also, the bodice length and the skirt length can be modified according to preference.

TIME:

Most girls can finish the entire dress, except for the hem, in 1½ hours.

PERSONAL PROGRESS GOALS:

Mia Maid 2, Choice and Accountability #2, assuming the dress will be worn with a blouse. Also, Mia Maid 1 and 2, Knowledge #1.

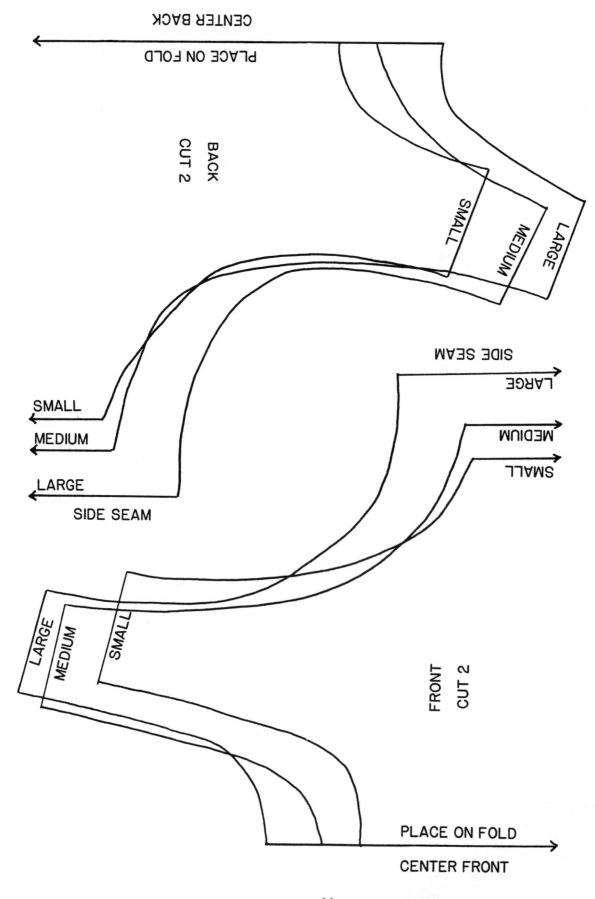

Choice and Accountability

Which Way to the Temple?

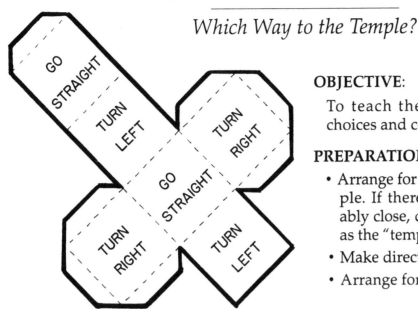

OBJECTIVE:

To teach the relationship between choices and consequences.

PREPARATION:

- Arrange for transportation to the temple. If there is not a temple reasonably close, designate another location as the "temple grounds."
- Make directions for the drivers.
- Arrange for a guest speaker.

PROCEDURE:

1. Divide the girls into carloads. Their goal is to arrive at the temple by a designated time. Give each team a paper cube (made from the pattern above) which is labeled with the words "turn right," "turn left," and "go straight." The teams toss this cube as they approach each intersection so that their routes are decided strictly by chance. (An envelope containing these instructions written on slips of paper could be used instead.) The driver follows the directions indicated on the cube. Obviously, all the cars will arrive in different places—none of which will be the temple—when the time is up. At that time, everyone goes to a designated spot by the temple.

2. While the girls are at the temple grounds, have a temple worker or other guest speaker compare the road trip to life. Have the speaker point out that, as the game demonstrated, no one will get to the temple by chance. The girls can only reach this goal by making the choices that will lead them there.

ALTERNATIVE:

Give each carload of girls a list of silly directions for making choices while they are en route to the temple. (Example: Find a red car and follow it for four blocks.) Involve the girls in creating the directions. On the other side of the directions, list requirements for temple recommend worthiness.

PERSONAL PROGRESS GOAL:

Ask the girls to select a Choice and Accountability goal that teaches the relationship between choices and consequences.

Choice and Accountability

Lesson Resources

ARTICLES

"But Why?" Paul J. Affleck, *New Era*, Mar. 1989, pp. 32-33. Dad couldn't give a reason for not wanting us to go, so we went.

"Enduring Mrs. Higgins," Claire Alyce Lund, *New Era*, Feb. 1992, pp. 26-27. Claire faced the consequences of her piano lessons.

"Hidden Choices," David C. Campbell, *New Era*, Oct. 1986, pp. 16-20. Like the policeman's bright green thermal underwear, our secrets will be exposed.

"Julie's Watching," Mary Ann Siggard, *New Era*, Jan. 1992, p. 29. A lovely non-member lost interest in the Church because of the actions of members.

"Make It Automatic," Richard G. Scott, *New Era*, Jan. 1992, p. 4. Some people run on automatic because of important decisions already made.

"Mushrooms, Music, Movies, and Magazines," Spencer J. Condie, *New Era*, Feb. 1990, pp. 4-6. Discerning the good ones from the bad ones affects our lives.

"Off Course," Donald Stokes, *New Era*, Feb. 1991, pp. 12-14. The twelve-year-old pilot remembered his father's instructions—for a while.

"Please Don't Give In," *New Era*, Sept. 1989, pp. 9-11. A former addict tells of the bitter fruits of his choices.

"Repentance," F. Burton Howard, *Ensign*, May 1991, pp. 12-14. We must not "justify our misconduct or blame others for our unhappiness."

"Surviving and Thriving in the 90s," Special Issue, *New Era*, Feb. 1990.

"Why Am I Running?" Angel Abrea, *New Era*, Jan. 1991, pp. 4-7. Do we use our agency or give it to others?

"Yagottawanna," Jack H. Goaslind, *New Era*, Feb. 1992, pp. 4-7. You have to want to do something before you will do it, and the consequences are eternal.

"You Turn," Loren C. Dunn, *New Era*, Jan. 1987, pp. 4-5. His grandfather, like us, came to a moment of decision, a "you-turn," that affected the rest of his life.

FICTION

"Pockets Full of Rocks," Larry Hiller, *New Era*, Mar. 1985, pp. 12-15. Story shows the absurdity and the consequence of carrying grudges.

MORMONADS

"Foul Language Is for the Birds," *New Era*, Apr. 1991, p. 15. Poster shows a boy and a parrot sitting in a tree.

"Little Vices Can Put You in a Big Squeeze," *New Era*, Feb. 1992, p. 37. Poster shows a young man caught in a c-clamp.

"Take Out the Trash," *New Era*, Apr. 1989, p. 27. Poster shows a young man emptying a garbage can out of his open head.

Choice and Accountability

Music Resources

HYMNS AND SONGS FOR YOUNG WOMEN OPENING EXERCISES

"Choose the Right" . . . . *Hymns*, no. 239
"Come Follow Me" . . . . *Hymns*, no. 116
"Do What Is Right" . . . . *Hymns*, no. 237
"Know This, That Every Soul Is Free" . . . . *Hymns*, no. 240
"Lord, I Would Follow Thee" . . . . *Hymns*, no. 220

AUDIO TAPES*

Songs	*Albums*
"A Lamp unto Your Feet"	*Hold to the Rod 7-12*
"Choices"	*Music for the Young Women Part A*
"Especially for Me"	*Music for the Young Women Part A*
"Free to Choose"	*Free to Choose*
"Hum Your Favorite Hymn"	*Music for the Young Women Part A*
"How Shall I Live?"	*Music for the Young Women Part B*
"I'll Trust in the Lord"	*Old Testament Media Songs*
"Look to God and Live"	*Hold to the Rod 7-12*
"To Bring Them to Thee"	*Old Testament Media Songs*
"Today"	*Old Testament Media Songs*
"Opposition"	*Music for the Young Women Part B*
"The Gift"	*Music for the Young Women Part B*
"The Voice of the Shepherd"	*Hold to the Rod 1-6*
"Tomorrow Has Promise"	*Music for the Young Women Part B*
"Up and Down"	*Music for the Young Women Part B*

MUSIC FOR SPECIAL NUMBERS

"Choices" . . . . *A Song of the Heart*, p. 40*
"Especially for Me" . . . . *A Song of the Heart*, p. 86
"Hum Your Favorite Hymn" . . . . *A Song of the Heart*, p. 89
"I'll Follow Christ" . . . . *New Era*, Aug. 1988, p. 12
"It Is with Christ" . . . . *New Era*, Aug. 1987, p. 50
"How Shall I Live?" . . . . *A Song of the Heart*, p. 20
"Opposition" . . . . *A Song of the Hear,t* p. 64
"The Gift" . . . . *A Song of the Heart*, p. 68
"Tomorrow Has Promise" . . . . *A Song of the Heart*, p. 90
"Up and Down" . . . . *A Song of the Heart*, p. 73

---

*Available from Church Distribution. *Free to Choose* and *Hold to the Rod* also available as songbooks. See page 109 of this book for details.

CHOOSE RIGHT OVER WRONG

Abraham 3:25-26

Words and Music by Jodi Johnston

Choose right o - ver
Choose right o - ver
Should you choose
Choose right o - ver

wrong.
wrong.
wrong,
wrong.

Choose to serve the Lord each
Pray each day to know His
Heav'n - ly Fa - ther will un - der -
Prove your val - iance here on the

day; we're here to prove our-selves.___ Safe - ty and___ peace.
will.___ This is why we're here: to choose right o - ver wrong.
stand. Re - pent and change your ways;___ His son has a - toned.
earth.___ You can pass the test;___ Choose right o - ver wrong.

for all e - ter - ni - ty for ev - ery child who will
We are ac - count - a -
Reach out and take His hand. This is why we're here– to
Do all that God com - mands. Peace and safe - ty fol - low.

ble_____ For

each choice that we make
A day will come when ev - ery child must

stand be - fore the Fa - ther and ac - count for each choice that we've made.

Free a - gen - cy is the Fa - ther's plan! Our bro - ther gave His life for each man!

"We will prove them here-with to see if they will do all things what-so-ev - er the Lord their God shall com - mand them, and they shall have glo-ry add-ed up-on their heads for-ev - er and ev - er." Glo-ry for-ev - er. Choose to fol-low all that God com-mands, Sa-tan's lies will ruin you. Choose right o - ver wrong.

D.S. al Coda   Coda

Rit.   D.S. al Coda   Coda Rit.

Rit.

Good Works

I will nurture others and build the kingdom through righteous service.

"Therefore let your light so shine before this people, that they may
see your good works and glorify your Father who is in heaven."

3 Nephi 12:16

Good Works

Car Window Wash

OBJECTIVE:

For the girls to serve many people in a simple way.

PREPARATION:

- Assign the girls to bring the materials listed below.
- Make copies of the handouts for the windshields (see the following page).

MATERIALS:

- Window cleaner
- Squeegees
- Towels

PROCEDURE:

Meet at a church or a school parking lot at a time when cars will be parked there. Have the girls wash the car windows.

EXAMPLE:

During a Cub Scout Pinewood Derby, the Beehives in one ward washed all the windows, not just the windshields, on all the cars in the parking lot. Afterwards, under the windshield wipers of each car, they left a note like those on the following page.

PERSONAL PROGRESS GOALS:

Beehive 2, Good Works #3; Mia Maid 1, Good Works #4 or #5; Mia Maid 2, Good Works #2.

Window wash compliments
of the Young Women

"Arise and shine forth
that thy light may be a
standard for the nations."

D&C 115:5

Window wash compliments
of the Beehive class

"Arise and shine forth
that thy light may be a
standard for the nations."

D&C 115:5

Window wash compliments
of the Mia Maid class

"Arise and shine forth
that thy light may be a
standard for the nations."

D&C 115:5

Window wash compliments
of the Laurel class

"Arise and shine forth
that thy light may be a
standard for the nations."

D&C 115:5

Good Works

Dinner for Singles

OBJECTIVE:

For the girls to serve dinner to the single members of the ward.

PREPARATION:

- Get approval to pay food expenses from the ward budget.
- Ask a specialist who has experience serving large group dinners to help plan and put the meal together.
- Deliver invitations to the guests (see the next page). Follow up with RSVPs.
- Make a place card for each guest.
- Arrange for food, entertainment, and decorations.

PROCEDURE:

Ask the Young Women to volunteer to cook the food in their homes. Have them choose and prepare the entertainment. Hold the dinner at the church and use tablecloths, nice dishes, and decorations.

EXAMPLE:

For one group of singles, the dinner was an important occasion for fellowshipping because many of those invited did not attend church regularly. The girls who brought and served their own single mom or dad enjoyed a bonding experience with that parent as well.

PERSONAL PROGRESS GOALS:

Beehive 2, Good Works #3; Mia Maid 1, Good Works #4 or #5; Mia Maid 2, Good Works #2. Suitable, with approval, for a Laurel project.

Place Card
(copy and fold in half)

You're Invited

To a special dinner

Date:

Time:

Place:

Food and entertainment
provided by the
ward Young Women

Please RSVP to:

Good Works

Educational Dominoes

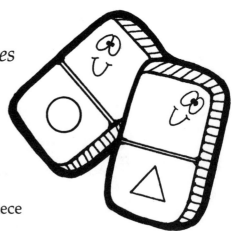

OBJECTIVES:

To help the girls make toys for children who live in a shelter and to learn how to make an educational toy.

PREPARATION:

- Purchase lumber measuring ¼" x 1¾ " x 7'. One piece makes one domino set.
- Mark the lumber at 3-inch intervals. Because of the width of the saw, if you skip this step, you will be short a piece. (If you purchase 8' lumber, this is not a problem.)
- Have someone cut the lumber with a band saw. Yield: 28 dominoes.
- Make copies of page 79 for the girls to work from.

MATERIALS:

- Domino pieces
- Clear acrylic spray
- Newspaper
- Stencils or cutout shapes one inch in size
- Permanent felt markers in 7 bright colors

PROCEDURE:

1. Make sure the girls check off each combination of shapes or colors on the following handout as they draw them on the dominoes. This will ensure that they have the right pieces when they are finished.
2. To make the shapes uniform in size, the girls may use stencils or cutouts, or they can carefully draw the shapes freehand with markers.
3. After the dominoes are made, take them outside, place them on newspaper, and spray them with clear acrylic so that the marker colors are permanent.
4. Donate the domino games to an emergency shelter for children.

SUGGESTION:

Point out that the dominoes can be used to teach shape recognition, a pre-reading readiness skill.

VARIATIONS:

Use rubber stamps and ink pads to make a more advanced set of dominoes. For example, a set of animal stamps can be used to teach children to distinguish smaller, more detailed shapes. Be sure that the impressions made with the stamps are large and clear enough to be seen easily. Test for permanency.

Card stock or poster board that is laminated can be used instead of wood. However, wood is recommended for durability.

PERSONAL PROGRESS GOALS:

Beehive 2, Good Works #3; Mia Maid 1, Good Works #4 or #5; Mia Maid 2, Good Works #2.

MAKE ONE DOMINO PER COMBINATION
OF COLORS OR SHAPES SHOWN BELOW:

Set 1—**Shapes**:

Make these dominoes using one color and different shapes. Check off the combinations as you make each domino.

__ square/circle
__ square/octagon
__ square/heart
__ square/oval
__ square/diamond
__ square/triangle
__ square/square

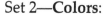

__ circle/circle
__ circle/octagon
__ circle/heart
__ circle/oval
__ circle/diamond
__ circle/triangle

__ octagon/octagon
__ octagon/heart
__ octagon/oval
__ octagon/diamond
__ octagon/triangle

__ heart/heart
__ heart/oval
__ heart/diamond
__ heart/triangle

__ oval/oval
__ oval/diamond
__ oval/triangle

__ diamond/diamond
__ diamond/triangle

__ triangle/triangle

Set 2—**Colors**:

Make these dominoes using one shape and different colors. Check off the combinations as you make each domino.

__ red/yellow
__ red/blue
__ red/green
__ red/purple
__ red/orange
__ red/brown
__ red/red

__ yellow/yellow
__ yellow/blue
__ yellow/green
__ yellow/purple
__ yellow/orange
__ yellow/brown

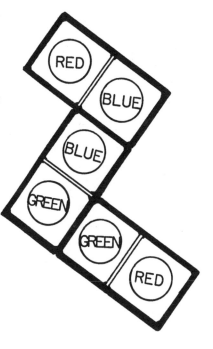

__ blue/blue
__ blue/green
__ blue/purple
__ blue/orange
__ blue/brown

__ green/green
__ green/purple
__ green/orange
__ green/brown

__ purple/purple
__ purple/orange
__ purple/brown

__ orange/orange
__ orange/brown

__ brown/brown

Good Works

Inlaid Foam Puzzles

OBJECTIVES:

For the girls to make toys for children in a shelter and to learn how to make an educational toy.

PREPARATION:

- Purchase closed-cell foam or if available, a solid color rubber kitchen mat.
- With a paper cutter, cut the foam to measure 9" x 12" or 12" x 16".
- Choose pictures carefully. Use the art on pages 81-83 or look through coloring books for simple pictures. Select pictures with simple outlines that can be used as patterns to cut around. Pieces should fit inside each other. Puzzle pieces of differing sizes and shapes will teach pre-reading readiness skills to children while they play.

MATERIALS:

- Exacto knives (preferred) or single edge razor blades
- Broad-tipped permanent felt markers in bright colors
- Clear acrylic spray   • Pictures
- Straight pins   • Cookie cutters (optional)

PROCEDURE:

1. Transfer the picture onto the foam by poking dots through the lines of the picture with a straight pin. Dots can be quite far apart. Carbon paper will not work because the foam is soft. (Optional method: copy pictures on card stock, cut the pieces apart, and trace around the pieces on the foam with a pen. To use this method, start with the pieces put together and remove them one by one as you trace around them.)
2. Cut out the puzzle using an Exacto knife. Cut carefully so the edges are smooth and fit together easily. Do not trim away any of the rough edges.
3. Color the pieces with permanent felt markers and spray them with acrylic.
4. Donate the puzzles to a shelter for children.

VARIATIONS:

Instead of a picture, use assorted cookie cutters, four to six on a puzzle. These should be all in one category in order to teach a single concept. For example, all the shapes could be animals. Press the cookie cutters into the foam and leave an indentation to follow to cut out the pieces. If desired, mount the puzzle frames onto another piece of foam or onto a piece of heavy cardboard.

EXAMPLE:

The girls in one Young Women's program enjoyed this activity and felt rewarded because they knew their efforts would help traumatized children.

PERSONAL PROGRESS GOALS:

Beehive 2, Good Works #3; Mia Maid 1, Good Works #4 and #5; Mia Maid 2, Good Works #2. Suitable, with expansion, for a Laurel project.

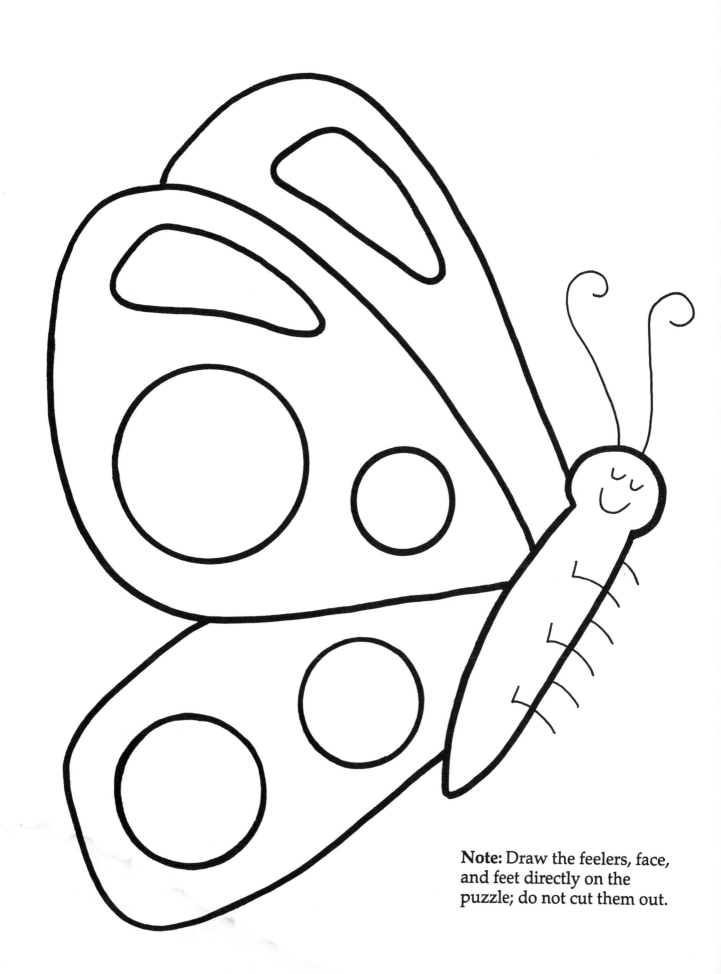

Note: Draw the feelers, face, and feet directly on the puzzle; do not cut them out.

Note: Draw the kite string directly on the puzzle; do not cut it out.

Note: Do not cut off the tail; leave it connected to the shell.

Good Works

Instead of "TP-ing"

OBJECTIVE:

For the girls to learn to be thoughtful of others.

MATERIALS:

- Construction paper or photocopies of art from pages 85-89 (as desired)
- 10" skewers (available in grocery stores)
- Marking pens
- Scissors
- Tape

PROCEDURE:

Cut out a huge stack of big, brightly colored hearts and tape each one onto a separate 10" wooden skewer. Decorate some and write messages on others. Instead of "TP-ing," the girls are ready for "hearting" some front yards. They simply stick the skewers in the lawn one by one at random. Some girls call this a "heart attack."

EXAMPLES:

- An 84-year-old widow was so pleased with the hearts placed in her yard that she left them there for several days.
- Bright paper hearts cheered up a lonely husband whose wife was out of town.
- Hearting encouraged some unemployed families.
- Hearting welcomed back a girl returning home from the hospital.
- Hearts helped a less active girl realize that her class missed her.
- Hearts pleasantly surprised one young woman on her birthday.
- One young man found his yard "hearted" as an invitation to a girl's choice dance.

VARIATIONS:

Other creative ideas for decorating yards have sprung from "hearting." One Beehive class "shamrocked" the house of an elderly man, to his delight. Later, they "egged" the house of a boyfriend with decorated paper Easter eggs. Another Beehive class "teepeed" a yard with paper teepee cutouts. Using a little imagination, young women can think of other clever variations for different people and occasions.

COMMENTS:

"Hearting," a positive alternative to "TP-ing," provides the same fun risk of discovery. Instead of a mess, the youth leave happiness behind. Both the youth and the recipients feel good. Girls involved in "hearting" have excitedly reported that "It's a lot of fun!"

PERSONAL PROGRESS GOALS:

Beehive 1, Good Works #8; Beehive 2, Good Works #3; Mia Maid 1, Good Works #5.

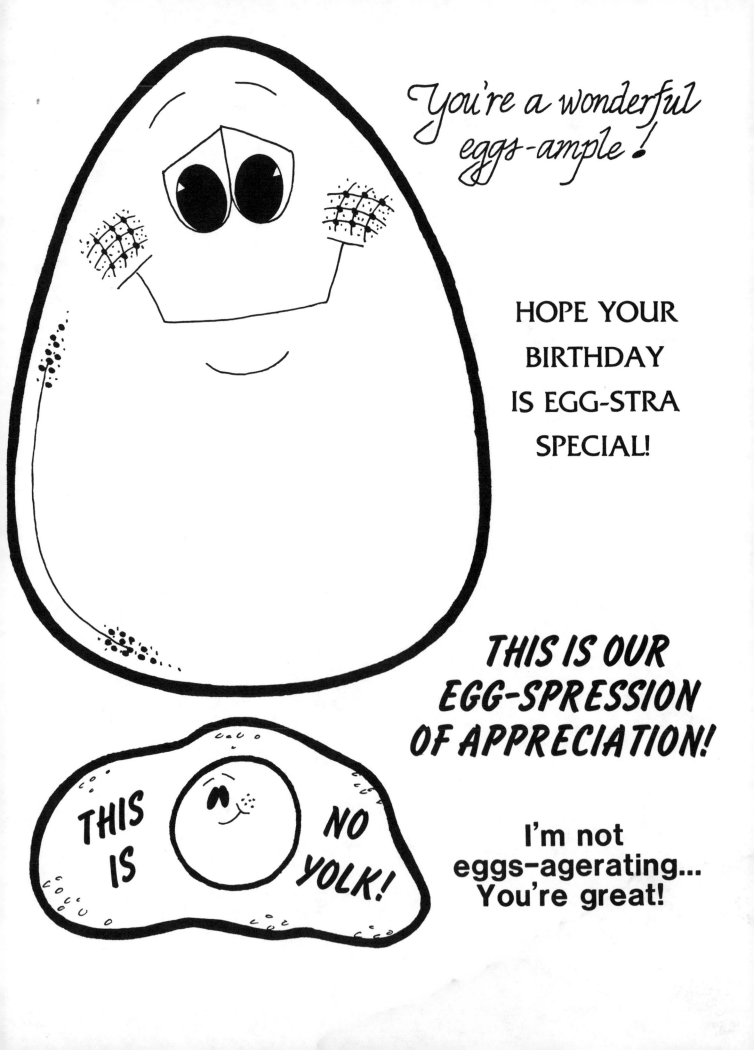

YOU ADD "SPARK" TO OUR CLASS!

Snap Crackle Pops!

You're just tops!

We just wanted to POP over and say HI!

I-rished for a friend and I found you!

ROSES ARE RED-
SHAMROCKS ARE GREEN-
WE JUST THINK
YOU'RE REALLY KEEN!

We have the luck o' the Irish 'cause you're in our class!

Good Works

Scripture Read-a-thon

OBJECTIVES:

To raise funds to donate to an approved cause and to motivate Young Women to read the Book of Mormon by committing them to a pledge program.

PREPARATION:

- Obtain your bishop's approval for the pledge program.
- Have the young women collect pledges for the number of pages they will read.

PROCEDURE:

Hold the Scripture Read-a-thon during a sleep-over and conduct activities during break periods. This can be a kick-off, wind-up, or one-time event.

EXAMPLE:

A girl in one Young Women's program completed her goal to read the entire Book of Mormon for this project.

COMMENTS:

This activity was submitted by a Mia Maid who chose it as the one she remembered and liked best.

PERSONAL PROGRESS GOALS:

Beehive 1, Faith #5; Beehive 2, Good Works #3; Mia Maid 1, Good Works #4 and #5; Mia Maid 2, Faith #9; Mia Maid 2, Good Works #2. Also suitable for a Laurel project.

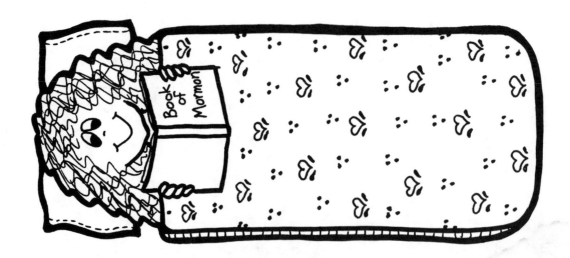

Good Works

Lesson Resources

ARTICLES

"A Handy Guide to Serving with Your Heart," Special Issue, *New Era*, March 1988.

"Giving Is Getting," D. Louise Brown, *New Era*, Dec. 1986, pp. 32-33. She spent her savings from the entire summer for her family's Christmas.

"Kindness—A Part of God's Plan," Betty Jo Jepsen, *Ensign*, Nov. 1990, pp. 91-92. Article includes examples of how kindness involves action.

"Signs of Hope," Anita M. Fee, *New Era*, Dec. 1989, pp. 36-37. A recipient of Donna's good works, she put jealousy aside to develop her own talents.

"Something in Return," Kirsten Andersen, *New Era*, Nov. 1989, p. 39. Kirsten realized she was doing secret deeds for her neighbor for the wrong reason.

"The Bus Stop," C. S. Hankins, *New Era*, Apr. 1991, pp. 26-27. Little acts of friendship led to conversion.

"The Necklace," Dayle King Searle, *New Era*, Dec. 1986, pp. 26-27. Her brother's happy face taught Dayle to think of others' feelings.

"The Service That Counts," Thomas S. Monson, *Ensign*, Nov. 1989, pp. 45-48. Article gives examples for and about youth.

"The Water Bucket," Sue Draper, *New Era*, Aug. 1987, pp. 12-13. One French lady realized that if she kept giving water away her pipes wouldn't freeze.

"The Write Prescription," Diane Brinkman, *New Era*, Oct. 1989, pp. 12-14. Sarah sent the sick six-year-old boy a letter every day to cheer him up.

"Three O'Clock Charity," Brian Heckert, *New Era*, Feb. 1991, pp. 26-27. Strangers with instinctive kindness helped a blind man board the subway.

"Willing Hands," Ann W. Moore, *New Era*, July 1989, pp. 12-15. She went with her family because she had to, only to discover that serving was fun.

FICTION

"Earl," Dian Saderup," *New Era*, Oct. 1989, pp. 48-50. After watching him at the nursing home, she realized her good works were full of self-righteousness.

MORMONADS

"Be a Smart Cookie," *New Era*, Feb. 1986, p. 13. Poster shows valentine cookies with messages of service and kindness.

"Get Yourself into a Tight Squeeze," *New Era*, Oct. 1988, p. 7. Poster shows a boy giving pansies and a hug to an older lady.

"Ready To Serve?" *New Era*, Feb. 1991, p. 7. Poster shows a tennis racket with a hole.

"Service—Get a Handle on It," *New Era*, June 1987. Poster-sized centerfold shows youth with hoe, rake, and paint brush without handles.

Good Works

Music Resources

HYMNS AND SONGS FOR YOUNG WOMEN OPENING EXERCISES

"Because I Have Been Given Much" . . . . *Hymns,* no. 219
"Called to Serve" . . . . *Hymns,* no. 249
"Have I Done Any Good?" . . . . *Hymns,* no. 223
"I Have Work Enough to Do" . . . . *Hymns,* no. 224
"I'll Go Where You Want Me to Go" . . . . *Hymns,* no. 270
"Improve the Shining Moments" . . . . *Hymns,* no. 226
"I Want to Live the Gospel" . . . . *Children's Songbook,* p. 148*
"Let Us All Press On" . . . . *Hymns,* no. 243
"Put Your Shoulder to the Wheel" . . . . *Hymns,* no. 252
"Scatter Sunshine" . . . . *Hymns,* no. 230
"Today, While the Sun Shines" . . . . *Hymns,* no. 229

AUDIO TAPES*

Songs	*Albums*
"Father, Lead Me Gently with Thy Love"	*Music for the Young Women Part B*
"Learning More of Love"	*Music for the Young Women Part A*
"Little Things"	*Music for the Young Women Part A*
"Look Inside"	*Music for the Young Women Part B*
"Sharing"	*Music for the Young Women Part A*
"The Little Things I Do"	*Music for the Young Women Part B*
"To Love, To Share, To Offer All"	*Music for the Young Women Part B*

MUSIC FOR SPECIAL NUMBERS

"Father, Lead Me Gently with Thy Love" . . . . *A Song of the Heart,* p. 43*
"Little Things" . . . . *A Song of the Heart,* p. 32
"Learning More of Love" . . . . *A Song of the Heart,* p. 50
"Look Inside" . . . . *A Song of the Heart,* p. 61
"Look Inside" . . . . *New Era,* Jan. 1992, p. 10
"Sharing" . . . . *A Song of the Heart,* p. 94
"The Little Things I Do" . . . . *A Song of the Heart,* p. 54
"To Love, To Share, To Offer All" . . . . *A Song of the Heart,* p. 4

*Available from Church Distribution. See page 109 of this book for details.

WHEN WE SERVE

Sincerely, with feeling

Words and Music by Daryl O. Smith

1. There are

times in our lives when we long for strength and to
live each day and we choose for His way, in-stru-

feel His love and peace._____ If we
ments of His and we'll be._____ When we

turn   our   hearts   to the   one   who   loves   He will

serve   our   friends   and our   fam - i - ly   His

gent - ly___   fill   our   needs._____   Through__

light   through our   love   we'll   see._____   Good__

times   of   strug - gle   when we   feel   a - lone,   His com-

works   of   ser - vice   to our   fel - low - men   build the

mand - ments   we   must   keep._____   There is

king - dom   and   bring   peace._____

one who knows all things;_____ Ways of

lift - ing oth - ers He brings._____ Our

Fa - ther a - bove wants us to love and serve each

oth - er will-ing - ly._____ Af - ter strife and

Integrity

*I have the moral courage to make my actions consistent
with my knowledge of right and wrong.*

"Till I die I will not remove mine integrity from me."

Job 27:5

Integrity

Balloon Lies

OBJECTIVES: To emphasize the importance of keeping lies out of our lives. To reinforce the color purple for integrity.

PREPARATION:
• Purchase and fill purple water balloons.
• Set up a volleyball net outdoors.
• Bring two bed sheets.

PROCEDURE: Split the girls into two teams. Give each team a bed sheet. The purple water balloons represent integrity. The teams take turns tossing the balloons back and forth over the volleyball net using their tightly stretched bed sheets. If the balloon (their integrity) breaks, the girls on one team get wet symbolizing what can happen when we get caught in a lie.

REFRESHMENTS: Purple popsicles.

Integrity

Integrity Ball

OBJECTIVE:

To show the girls that when we face opposition, we can keep ourselves clean and unspotted by maintaining our integrity.

PREPARATION:

- Locate a grassy field where the activity can be held.
- Assign the girls to wear old clothes that can get wet and dirty.
- Assign the girls to bring towels and Personal Progress books.

MATERIALS:

- One bat and one soccer ball
- 4 large plastic cups, all of the same size
- 4 five-gallon containers full of water
- 4 waterproof bases
- 4 sturdy oversized raincoats

PROCEDURE:

1. On a grassy field, place the bases as you would for a softball game. Set a 5-gallon container of water and a large plastic cup on the outside of each base, including home.

2. The batter, who wears a raincoat, kicks the ball and runs to as many bases as she can. Meanwhile, using the cups, the basemen try to douse the runner with water. Obviously, the raincoat, which symbolizes integrity, will protect the runner from the "dangers" that cross her path until she can get to safety.

3. If the opposition stops the runner, she loses her protection. She must take off the raincoat, wad it up, and carry it with her to the remaining bases; she cannot use it as a shield. Without her integrity, the runner will likely get drenched by the waters of "temptation."

4. Runners who lose the raincoat receive one point when they reach home. These players can use the towels to dry off (to "repent"). Those arriving safely home still wearing a raincoat earn two points because they have maintained their integrity in a treacherous world.

5. Outs are made in the usual way.

SUGGESTION:

Explain the symbolism of the game before beginning. When you finish, gather the girls together and ask them what home base symbolizes. Help them realize that some day "home base" will be our heavenly home and that we will arrive either "wet" or "dry" after our sojourn in life, depending on our level of integrity and righteousness. Also, help them understand that the towels represent repentance and that when we apply this principle, we can become "dry" again. Encourage the girls to keep their raincoats of integrity on throughout their lives.

Note: This experience should be held on a weekday following a Sunday discussion on integrity so the girls more fully understand what the word means.

VARIATION:

If you have a convenient water source at the field, use clean, 32-gallon trash cans instead of five-gallon containers and 2-quart pitchers instead of cups.

SCRIPTURE:

"My lips shall not speak wickedness, nor my tongue utter deceit. . . . till I die *I will not remove mine integrity from me*. My righteousness I hold fast, and will not let it go." (Job 27:4-6; italics added.)

PERSONAL PROGRESS GOALS:

End the experience by giving the girls a few minutes to set a Personal Progress Integrity goal that will help them practice the ideas they learned in this experience.

"Water" you doing? "soak" up

Come to Mutual and some fun!

Date:

Time:

Place:

Integrity

Integrity in the Park

OBJECTIVE:

To encourage the girls to develop more integrity.

PREPARATION:

- Assign the girls to bring a story to share that illustrates integrity.
- Assign the girls to bring a food that is mentioned in the scriptures.
- Bring a camping lantern.

PROCEDURE:

Drive to a nearby park. Have the girls sit in a circle on the grass around a lighted lantern and share stories that illustrate integrity.

EXAMPLE:

In this setting, one Mia Maid class shared special closeness as they sat in a circle as if around a campfire. When one girl shared her food, her advisor laughingly asked, "Where is pizza mentioned in the scriptures?"

SUGGESTION:

Eating food that is mentioned in the scriptures will match the activity if the stories discussed are also from the scriptures.

VARIATIONS:

At the end of the evening, allow the girls some time to set a goal that will help them develop integrity. Or, have them set a goal two weeks before the activity and then tell about their experiences as they worked to achieve the goal. Most of the goals listed below could be used in this way.

PERSONAL PROGRESS GOALS:

Beehive 1,
Integrity #2, #3,
#5, and #6;
Beehive 2,
Integrity #1, #2, #3,
#4, #7, and #8;
Mia Maid 1,
Integrity #2, #3, #4,
#5, #6, #7, and #8;
Mia Maid 2,
Integrity #3 and #5.

101

Integrity

Mock Jury Trial

OBJECTIVE:

To illustrate that our integrity is on trial daily.

PREPARATION:

Assign the girls their roles ahead of time so they have time to prepare.

PROCEDURE:

Conduct a mock trial using the following example or a case study the girls write. The witnesses should tell different versions of the story. After the jury makes a decision, reveal what actually happened.

"The Case of the Missing Keys"

SITUATION:

A boys' P.E. class and a girls' P.E. class were outside playing volleyball. After class, the boys' coach, Mr. McConnell, needed to put the nets away. Because Mr. McConnell left his keys inside, he sent Clint to ask the girls' coach, Ms. Adams, if he could borrow her keys. After she gave her keys to Clint, he and a few other boys put the nets away. In the process, Clint handed the keys to Brian to carry. Before long, Ms. Adams needed her keys, so she sent Erica to get them. Clint retrieved the keys from Brian and gave them to Erica, who then gave them to her coach. A few minutes later, Ms. Adams noticed that the towel room key was missing. This key was important because although it did not open any other doors, it did open the door to the towel room, which led into the girls' locker room.

SUSPECTS:

Erica:

Erica is a good student who attends seminary. Well-known for her sense of humor, she loves to play jokes on people. At an honor assembly held the night before the key disappeared, she was passed over for an award that she was supposed to receive from the P.E. department. She felt embarrassed over the incident.

Clint:

Clint is a B student who ditches seminary occasionally. Earlier on the day the key disappeared, a teacher caught him using a fake pass. Just before he received the keys, he watched the girls' coach, Ms. Adams, locking the towel room door.

Brian:

Brian is an average student who is not a member of the Church. He has a history of minor offenses at school, such as mouthing off. He detests the extra laps his P.E. teacher makes him run when he is late. He had the keys the longest.

Verdict:

In this actual incident (names changed), Clint was the guilty party. While he had Ms. Adams' keys, Clint took the towel room key off the key ring and hid it in the grass. Neither Brian nor Erica knew what had happened. Afterwards, the principal told Erica that he believed she was innocent because he knew she had high standards. She was a young woman of integrity.

Integrity

Values in Counted Cross-stitch

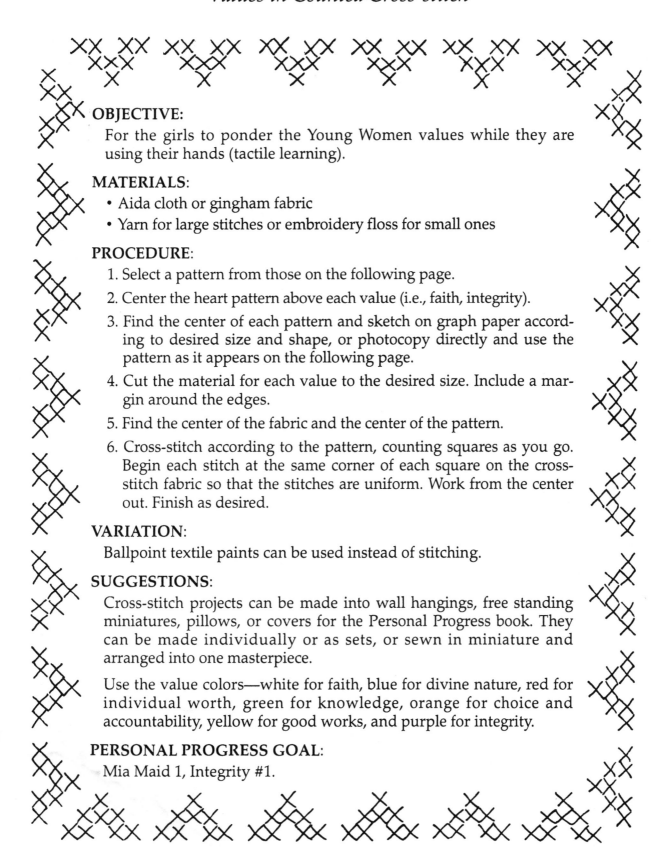

OBJECTIVE:

For the girls to ponder the Young Women values while they are using their hands (tactile learning).

MATERIALS:

- Aida cloth or gingham fabric
- Yarn for large stitches or embroidery floss for small ones

PROCEDURE:

1. Select a pattern from those on the following page.

2. Center the heart pattern above each value (i.e., faith, integrity).

3. Find the center of each pattern and sketch on graph paper according to desired size and shape, or photocopy directly and use the pattern as it appears on the following page.

4. Cut the material for each value to the desired size. Include a margin around the edges.

5. Find the center of the fabric and the center of the pattern.

6. Cross-stitch according to the pattern, counting squares as you go. Begin each stitch at the same corner of each square on the cross-stitch fabric so that the stitches are uniform. Work from the center out. Finish as desired.

VARIATION:

Ballpoint textile paints can be used instead of stitching.

SUGGESTIONS:

Cross-stitch projects can be made into wall hangings, free standing miniatures, pillows, or covers for the Personal Progress book. They can be made individually or as sets, or sewn in miniature and arranged into one masterpiece.

Use the value colors—white for faith, blue for divine nature, red for individual worth, green for knowledge, orange for choice and accountability, yellow for good works, and purple for integrity.

PERSONAL PROGRESS GOAL:

Mia Maid 1, Integrity #1.

Integrity

Lesson Resources

ARTICLES

"A Marvelous Work," Chris Crowe, *New Era*, Feb. 1987, pp. 32-35. Although in tears, Liz, who didn't want to compromise her values, broke up with her nonmember boyfriend by handing him a Mormon book. Special issue on "Courtship and Marriage."

"Away From the Blinding Dust," M. Russell Ballard, *New Era*, May 1991, pp. 44-50. A General Authority gives steps to take to remain morally clean.

"How to Say No and Keep Your Friends," Chris Crowe, *New Era*, Feb. 1988, pp. 8-11. Your answer will affect how you and your friends feel about you.

"My Reputation," Teresa B. Clark, *New Era*, June 1990, pp. 48-50. She led a double life.

"One Who Did," Barbara Merrell, *New Era*, Aug. 1987, pp. 38-39. When the hostess wouldn't watch an R-rated video, the others changed their minds.

"Q&A: Don't Circumstances Sometimes Determine What's Right and Wrong?" *New Era*, Sept. 1991, pp. 16-19. I can't compete if I don't cheat.

"Q&A: How Can I Bring Myself to Confess to the Bishop?" *New Era*, Oct. 1989, pp. 16-19.

"Q&A: What Can I Do [So] I Won't Give In?" *New Era*, July 1990. pp. 16-19.

"Stretching the Truth," Lynn Mickelsen, *New Era*, Apr. 1992, pp. 4-7. Our point of refusal determines our integrity. Article includes pictures of girl with Pinocchio nose.

"The Best Policy," Keith W. Wilcox, *New Era*, Nov. 1986, pp. 4-7. His life was spared because he truthfully, although reluctantly, marked "yes" on the form.

"The Enemy in the Gutter," John Bytheway, *New Era*, Mar. 1992, pp. 8-9. The opponent was eleven inches tall, a pornographic magazine.

"The Goal Keeper," Lisa A. Johnson, *New Era*, Feb. 1990, pp. 32-34. Even with intense pressure, she stood up for her convictions.

"What Am I Doing Wrong?" Carl Houghton, *New Era*, Sept. 1987, p. 12. Carl read the scriptures, realizing that they weren't affecting his actions.

"When the Pressure Is On," Stephanie Christensen, *New Era*, Jan. 1988, pp. 8-9. Stephanie was the only one who refused to go along with the plan.

FICTION

"Let Them Eat Figs," Jack Weyland, *New Era*, Oct. 1991, p. 32. Ryan's strange dream of passing tests to heroically win a medieval kingdom suddenly made sense in real life.

MORMONADS

"Don't Fall For It," *New Era*, May 1991, p. 14. Poster shows dominoes, with faces on them, that have knocked each other over except for one standing firm.

"In Case of Temptation," *New Era*, June 1992, p. 19. Running shoes are kept behind glass of fire alarm box.

Integrity

Music Resources

HYMNS AND SONGS FOR YOUNG WOMEN OPENING EXERCISES

"Carry On" . . . . *Hymns*, no. 255

"Dare to Do Right" . . . . *Children's Songbook*, p. 158

"I Pledge Myself to Love the Right" . . . . *Children's Songbook*, p. 161

"Keep the Commandments" . . . . *Hymns*, no. 303

"Love One Another" . . . . *Hymns*, no. 308

"Stand for the Right" . . . . *Children's Songbook*, p. 159

"The Iron Rod" . . . . *Hymns*, no. 274

"The Temple Is a Sacred Place" . . . . *Sing With Me*, p. B-31*

"True to the Faith" . . . . *Hymns*, no. 254

"Who's on the Lord's Side" . . . . *Hymns*, no. 260

AUDIO TAPES**

Songs	*Albums*
"A Little at a Time"	*Music for the Young Women Part B*
"Behold Thy Handmaiden"	*Music for the Young Women Part A*
"Behold Thy Handmaiden" (simplified)	*Music for the Young Women Part B*
"Create an Atmosphere"	*Music for the Young Women Part B*
"Follow His Way"	*Music for the Young Women Part B*
"Hold to the Rod" (instrumental)	*Hold to the Rod 1-6*
"Honest and Truthfully Yours"	*Music for the Young Women Part A*
"Let Me Soar"	*Music for the Young Women Part A*
"Promises"	*Music for the Young Women Part A*

MUSIC FOR SPECIAL NUMBERS

"A Little at a Time" . . . . *A Song of the Heart*, p. 76**

"A Mighty Wave" . . . . *New Era*, Oct. 1986, p. 10

"Behold Thy Handmaiden" . . . . *A Song of the Heart*, p. 104

"Behold Thy Handmaiden" (simplified) . . . . *A Song of the Heart*, p. 114

"Create an Atmosphere" . . . . *A Song of the Heart*, p. 56

"Follow His Way" . . . . *A Song of the Heart*, p. 24

"Honest and Truthfully Yours" . . . . *A Song of the Heart*, p. 82

"If You Love 'Em, Tell 'Em" . . . . *New Era*, Oct. 1987, p. 12

"Let Me Soar" . . . . *A Song of the Heart*, p. 9

"Promises" . . . . *A Song of the Heart*, p. 84

---

*Discontinued from Church Distribution.

**Available from Church Distribution. Hold to the Rod also available as a songbook. See
page 109 of this book for details.

BE TRUE

For the Strength of Youth
Sincerely

Words and Music by Kaimi Wenger

1. Be true to your-self and the joy that you find will
true to man-kind ev' - ry - where that you go and you'll

shine like a bea - con with - in, For truth is the key to un -
find you are greet - ed with trust. Your good rep - u - ta - tion will

1

lock - ing your mind and a shield to pro - tect you from sin. 2. Be
flour - ish and grow if___

2

all of your deal - ings are just. Be true to your God and the

bless - ings He gives will leave you no room to re - ceive. He'll

lead you and guide you as long as you live if you but en - dure and be -

lieve. Be true in your thoughts, in your words, in your deeds, and

in ev' - ry - thing that you do, And you will be saved in the

King - dom of God if you can be - lieve and be true.

Church Distribution Resources

Manual

Gospel Principles..order #31110 $2.00

The following tapes can be ordered from Church Distribution for $1.00 each:

Free to Choose (seminary—Book of Mormon).........................order #52440

Hold to the Rod 1-6 (seminary—scripture motivation)...............order #52442

Hold to the Rod 7-12 (seminary— scripture motivation)..............order #52443

Music for the Young Women Part A (vocal)........................order #52057

Music for the Young Women Part B (vocal).........................order #52058

Music for the Young Women Part A (instrumental)..................order #52084

Music for the Young Women Part B (instrumental)..................order #52085

Music from Young Women Firesides, 1985 and 1987..................order #52298

New Testament Media Songs (seminary) ....order #53486

Old Testament Media Songs (seminary) ....order #52451

Selected Hymns (instrumental) (set of 6 tapes for $6.00) ....order #52427

   Note: Series A correlates with Course A manuals and Series B with Course B manuals.

Printed Music

A Song of the Heart (Young Women songbook, "the purple book") order #32509 $2.75

Children's Songbook (Primary songbook—hardbound) ....order #31246 $6.25

Children's Songbook (Primary songbook—spiral)................order #33441 $6.25

Come, Hold Your Torches High (sheet music).....................order #32510 $ .35

Free to Choose Songbook (seminary)............................order #32343 $1.50

Hold to the Rod Songbook (seminary)...........................order #32718 $1.00

Order by Mail

Salt Lake City Distribution Center, 1999 West 1700 South, Salt Lake City, Utah 84104. For orders of less than $25, add $2.25 postage and handling. Utah residents add sales tax. Make checks payable to Corporation of the President.

Order by Phone

240-5274 (Salt Lake area) or 1-800-537-5950 (toll free long distance in U.S. and Canada). There is a $2.00 service charge on phone orders.